NARRATIVE INQUIRERS IN THE MIDST OF MEANING-MAKING: INTERPRETIVE ACTS OF TEACHER EDUCATORS

ADVANCES IN RESEARCH ON TEACHING

Series Editor: Volumes 1–11: Jere Brophy
Volumes 12–15: Stefinee Pinnegar

Recent Volumes

Volume 1:	Teachers for Understanding and Self Regulation
Volume 2:	Teacher Knowledge of Subject Matter
Volume 3:	Planning and Managing Learning Tasks
Volume 4:	Case Studies of Teaching and Learning
Volume 5:	Learning and Teaching Elementary Subjects
Volume 6:	Teaching and Learning History
Volume 7:	Expectations in the Classroom
Volume 8:	Subject-Specific Instructional Methods and Activities
Volume 9:	Social Constructivist Teaching: Affordances and Constraints
Volume 10:	Using Video in Teacher Education
Volume 11:	Learning From Research on Teaching: Perspective, Methodology and Representation
Volume 12:	Tensions in Teacher Preparation: Accountability, Assessment, and Accreditation
Volume 13:	Narrative Inquiries into Curriculum Making in Teacher Education
Volume 14:	Places of Curriculum Making: Narrative Inquiries into Children's Lives in Motion
Volume 15:	Adolescent Boys' Literate Identity

ADVANCES IN RESEARCH ON TEACHING   VOLUME 16

NARRATIVE INQUIRERS IN THE MIDST OF MEANING-MAKING: INTERPRETIVE ACTS OF TEACHER EDUCATORS

EDITED BY

ELAINE CHAN
University of Nebraska-Lincoln, Nebraska

DIXIE KEYES
Arkansas State University, Arkansas

VICKI ROSS
Northern Arizona University, Arizona

Emerald

United Kingdom – North America – Japan
India – Malaysia – China

Emerald Group Publishing Limited
Howard House, Wagon Lane, Bingley BD16 1WA, UK

First edition 2012

Copyright © 2012 Emerald Group Publishing Limited

Reprints and permission service
Contact: booksandseries@emeraldinsight.com

No part of this book may be reproduced, stored in a retrieval system, transmitted in any form or by any means electronic, mechanical, photocopying, recording or otherwise without either the prior written permission of the publisher or a licence permitting restricted copying issued in the UK by The Copyright Licensing Agency and in the USA by The Copyright Clearance Center. No responsibility is accepted for the accuracy of information contained in the text, illustrations or advertisements. The opinions expressed in these chapters are not necessarily those of the Editor or the publisher.

British Library Cataloguing in Publication Data
A catalogue record for this book is available from the British Library

ISBN: 978-1-78052-924-0
ISSN: 1479-3687 (Series)

ISOQAR certified Management Systems, awarded to Emerald for adherence to Quality and Environmental standards ISO 9001:2008 and 14001:2004, respectively

Certificate Number 1985
ISO 9001
ISO 14001

INVESTOR IN PEOPLE

CONTENTS

LIST OF CONTRIBUTORS	vii
ACKNOWLEDGEMENTS	ix
FOREWORD: CREATING OPENINGS TO PONDER INTERPRETATION, INCONCLUSIVITY, AND THE GEOGRAPHY OF NARRATIVE *Mary Lynn Hamilton*	xi
INTRODUCING BRAIDED RIVERS *Dixie Keyes, Vicki Ross and Elaine Chan*	xvii
CHAPTER ONE OPENNESS AND INCONCLUSIVITY IN INTERPRETATION IN NARRATIVE INQUIRY: DIMENSIONS OF THE SOCIAL/PERSONAL *Stefinee Pinnegar and Mary Lynn Hamilton*	1
CHAPTER TWO BURROWING AND BROADENING IN THE STORIED PLACE OF TEACHER EDUCATION *Dixie Keyes and Cheryl Craig*	23
CHAPTER THREE ATTENDING TO THE TEMPORAL DIMENSION OF NARRATIVE INQUIRY INTO TEACHER EDUCATOR IDENTITIES *M. Shaun Murphy, Vicki Ross and Janice Huber*	51
CHAPTER FOUR EXPLORING CHRONOTOPIC SHIFTS BETWEEN KNOWN AND UNKNOWN IN OUR TEACHER EDUCATOR IDENTITY NARRATIVES *Mary Rice and Cathy Coulter*	77

CHAPTER FIVE   CROSS-CULTURAL
INTERPRETATION OF FIELD TEXTS
   Candace Schlein and Elaine Chan   *109*

HEADWATERS AND TRIBUTARIES: MEANING-
MAKING USING THE THREE-DIMENSIONAL
NARRATIVE INQUIRY SPACE
   Vicki Ross, Elaine Chan and Dixie Keyes   *131*

AFTERWORD: REFLECTIONS ON NARRATIVE
INQUIRIES INTO TEACHER EDUCATION IDENTITY
MAKING
   D. Jean Clandinin   *143*

ABOUT THE CONTRIBUTORS   *149*

LIST OF CONTRIBUTORS

Elaine Chan	Department of Teaching, Learning, and Teacher Education, College of Education and Human Sciences, University of Nebraska-Lincoln, Lincoln, NE, USA
D. Jean Clandinin	Centre for Research for Teacher Education and Development, University of Alberta, Edmonton, AB, Canada
Cathy Coulter	College of Education, University of Alaska Anchorage, Anchorage, AK, USA
Cheryl Craig	Department of Curriculum and Instruction, University of Houston, Houston, TX, USA
Mary Lynn Hamilton	Curriculum and Teaching, School of Education, University of Kansas, Lawrence, KS, USA
Janice Huber	Faculty of Education, University of Regina, Regina, SK, Canada
Dixie Keyes	Department of Teacher Education, Arkansas State University, Jonesboro, AR, USA
M. Shaun Murphy	Curriculum Studies, University of Saskatchewan, Saskatoon, SK, Canada
Stefinee Pinnegar	Department of Teacher Education, McKay School of Education, Brigham Young University, Provo, UT, USA
Mary Rice	Teacher Education/Teaching English Language Learners (TELL), Brigham Young University, Springville, UT, USA

Vicki Ross   Department of Teaching and Learning, Northern Arizona University, Flagstaff, AZ, USA

Candace Schlein   School of Education, Division of Curriculum and Instructional Leadership, University of Missouri–Kansas City, Kansas City, MO, USA

ACKNOWLEDGEMENTS

We offer this book to our fellow narrativists, who share our appreciation for the nuances of a lively conversation about the intricacies of research methodology, and the beauty of the ebb and flow of a journey downriver.

Elaine:
I would like to acknowledge my husband, Morris, for his love and support, and for the care he takes to keep our family going when Mommy is huddled over work at the computer, and to my daughters, Alexandra and Lauren, who make my world go around.

Vicki:
I want to thank my husband, Bruce, and my daughters, Elissa and Hayley, for their support and encouragement. They make so much in my life possible. Also, I thank Dr. Michael Connelly, my teacher. His is the voice I hear in my head.

Dixie:
I would like to thank all of the members and friends in the AERA Narrative Research SIG for the constant encouragement, feedback and opportunities. And, what we do without artists and photographers? They bring life to our metaphors and to the images we rely on for our meaning-making. A special thanks to Dr. Bob Kelly for all of the photographs in this book and to sixth grade science teacher (and artist) Erica Sockwell for the lovely artwork found in the chapter dialogues.

FOREWORD: CREATING OPENINGS TO PONDER INTERPRETATION, INCONCLUSIVITY, AND THE GEOGRAPHY OF NARRATIVE

Mary Lynn Hamilton

Teacher educators, their pedagogy and their practice have garnered more attention within the past 10 years with suggestions to standardize expectations, generate pedagogical tools, explore practice, and more. Prior to that time, few researchers turned their attention in this direction. (Clandinin & Connelly and Cochran-Smith and Lytle are a few exceptions.) What this pedagogy includes and how to explore its enactment and ways to reveal the knowledge and identity of the teacher educators involved seems to call an increasing number of researchers to study these issues in teaching and teacher education. While some researchers attempt to put a fine point on the what and the how of these issues, they cannot easily reduce these experiences into a few simple exemplars. Instead, the experiences of teacher educators are unpolished, unsettled, uncertain, and unpredictable. Often, the idea of research is presented as orderly and linear for the purposes of conveying information and the results appear as a list of points to follow, but the lives of teacher educators and teachers and students are *not* so restricted or clear or certain. Rather, there can be almost a chaotic quality to those lives, which in turn, can reveal the beauty and the depth of the story and experience.

    This potentiality for the uncertain and unpredictable requires a steady-handed and thoughtful researcher to insure the integrity of the research. This is particularly true for those researchers engaged in narrative inquiry. These researchers must bring rigor and the commitment to trustworthiness as they attempt to reveal the plotlines and knowledge that is often ambiguous. It was their commitment to narrative inquiry, to rigor, and to the stories and knowledge of teachers and teacher educators that brought the authors in this text to write their chapters. From the beginning of this project, the authors set out to reveal their analytical and interpretive processes used in narrative inquiry to explore teacher educator identity and to demonstrate their moves from field texts to insights and wonderings about this identity. They engaged in practice as teacher educators and have developed their personal practical knowledge of teaching and teacher education in this role. While the authors include autobiographical narratives or stories of being teacher educators in practice, identify experiences that resonate with understanding of self as teacher educators, and offer discussions of interim field text, these chapters also highlight particular aspects of the three-dimensional narrative space (Clandinin & Connelly, 2000). In their chapters, these authors guide us through their processes to help us consider our own understandings of narrative inquiry.

MEANING-MAKING THROUGH METAPHOR

Geography has always drawn me like a magnet or an artist or a lover. In real or virtual life I can always see the textures and feel the metaphors. So when I saw the picture of the braided river, the image used by the editors as a way to enter into the text, *Narrative Inquirers in the Midst of Meaning-making: Interpretive Acts of Teacher Educators*, I sat quietly opening my mind to possibilities. Like a magnet my eyes held fast to the picture, like an artist I imagined colors, like a lover the image created desire to see more. Yet, the cranes called me as well with the huge wingspan, regal stance and red crowns. I could see the birds dancing through the braids, hovering upon the sands, sinking into the water.

Although unique, these braided rivers span the globe – from Alaska to Nebraska to New Zealand to British Columbia to Kyrgyzstan. These rivers are mobile and ever-changing with variable currents even from the outside to the inside of its curve. Like the sandhill cranes, these rivers have been around a long time. Like these rivers, the sandhill cranes are unpredictable and variable. Teacher educators are familiar with these sorts of changeability and experiences in their classrooms and their practice.

In the midst of my imagining, I saw the chapter authors fly and hop and twirl, certain in the uncertainty and power of the work they do. In this text the authors attempt to make visible the pull, the color and the desire of being teacher educators, making meaning of practice to help their students make meaning of their practice. Our meaning-making can be as messy like the mud along a braided river. Like a first look at the braiding rivers with

Foreword xiii

the dancing cranes clarity in plotline or knowledge is not always apparent. The use of metaphor serves meaning-making in narrative inquiry in several ways. As narrative inquirers, a metaphor can open the imagery of story that may be hidden from us by memory or experience or trauma. As one idea comes alongside another, the braids and cranes of a metaphor may separate or combine in ways that allow us to see what we have not seen previously. Metaphors also support readers' entry into a text because they recognize the braids and cranes – or reject them, yet follow along as they are intrigued by the use of the metaphor itself. In this text, the authors attempt to make visible analytic and interpretive choices in narrative inquiry to provide examples for colleagues of the process and the methodological thinking.

ISSUES TO CONSIDER

Some researchers have examined the relationship to teacher educators' identity as teachers and others have explored the elements of practice that reveal and account for elements of that identity. This research parallels and builds upon earlier work (e.g., Clandinin, Davies, Hogan, & Kennard, 1993) developed out of understandings that teachers' stories reveal teacher identities since that identity is evident in their stories of teaching and themselves as teachers. Examining stories offers glimpses of ways that a narrative approach with a deliberative stance may contribute to an enhanced awareness of the nuances of teacher knowledge and professional identity development. Examining the ways researchers might interpret those stories helps them think more deeply about the development of identities as teacher educators. Schwab's (1983) consideration of the role of deliberation in the planning and implementation of curriculum, Dewey's (1938) theory of experience as a foundation for learning, and Connelly and Clandinin's (1988) work on teacher knowledge and the role of experience in developing curriculum provide a theoretical foundation for this piece.

Critique of the value of narrative research often centers on issues of whether the process of meaning-making is a plotline of meaning-making. Such critiques may hold a secret story that narrative researchers begin with answers and then merely sift through stories to identify one that illustrates the answer they desire to assert. While narrative researchers may articulate, name and provide evidence for their meaning-making processes, those who have not engaged in this kind of meaning-making may not understand such a process, the depth of analysis engaged in, or the rigor of such examination. Whereas narrative inquirers and their participants worry about over-interpretation – or reading too much into the dailiness of their work, other researchers may consider stories of experience under-interpreted or under-theorized. In this text, authors provide demonstrations of this interpretive process to support new scholars learning it and more seasoned scholars interested in seeing collaborative meaning-making unfold.

These authors engage in practices as teacher educators and have developed personal practical knowledge of teaching and teacher education in this role. While the chapter authors have written autobiographical narratives or a story of being teacher educators in practice, identified experiences that resonate with understanding of self as teacher educators, and offered discussions of interim field text, each chapter highlights particular aspects of the three-dimensional narrative space (Clandinin & Connelly, 2000).

These authors demonstrate interpretation using the three-dimensional narrative space, unpacking and uncovering the meanings in the field texts. They examine *place* as they bring alongside personal contexts in contrast and support of the narrative and relevant literature. Regarding *temporality*, they consider today and the future as well as the past in terms of the context of teacher education within which teacher educator identity is formulated. As they move to sociality they lay issues of the personal and *social* alongside place and temporality to tease out meaning and make connections to the research literature. In the looking-alongside process, they take the opportunity to explore tensions between other field texts and the ones they place at center stage. In the chapter dialogues and in the last round of interpretation, they highlight the places where the past, present and future connect in ways that reinterpret the past and cause a reimagining of a future to renegotiate the present of both narrative inquiry and teacher educator identity.

Each chapter stands in the present moment intentionally engaging the zone of inconclusivity (Bakhtin, 1981) to bring together the past, present, and future in ways that destabilize interpretation and push meaning forward. The resulting uncertainty invites readers into further and deeper inquiry into the teacher educator identity and narrative inquiry methodology. As the authors make visible the process of developing narrative understanding, they hope to demonstrate the virtue and value of meaning-making in narrative inquiry and uncover the plotlines of teacher educator identity. All of this occurs "in the midst" of our thinking, our research, our lives, and our meaning-making of the lives we lead and the lives we connect (or do not) with as narrative inquirers.

This text takes up the methodology of narrative inquiry. Using the theoretical framework offered by three-dimensional narrative space, the chapters represent a departure for discussion about research methodology and teacher educator identity. Like the braided river that supports the sandhill cranes, providing sustenance and protection, I hope you find this book a source for guidance and illustration in your engagement with narrative inquiry.

REFERENCES

Bakhtin, M. (1981). *The dialogic imagination: Four essays*. Austin, TX: University of Texas Press.
Clandinin, D. J., & Connelly, F. M. (2000). *Narrative inquiry: Experience and story in qualitative research*. San Francisco, CA: Jossey-Bass.
Clandinin, D. J., Davies, A., Hogan, P., & Kennard, B. (1993). *Learning to teach, teaching to learn: Stories of collaboration in teacher education*. New York, NY: Teachers' College Press.
Connelly, F. M., & Clandinin, D. J. (1988). *Teachers as curriculum planners: Narratives of experience*. New York, NY: Teachers College Press.
Dewey, J. (1938). *Experience and education*. New York, NY: Simon & Schuster.
Schwab, J. J. (1983). The practical 4: Something for curriculum professors to do. *Curriculum Inquiry, 13*, 239–265.

INTRODUCING BRAIDED RIVERS

Dixie Keyes, Vicki Ross and Elaine Chan

We invite readers to join us on a journey of exploration and discovery as narrative inquirers and as teacher educators. As editors and chapter authors, our purpose in compiling this book was to explore, in what we hope are fairly explicit ways, the processes of making meaning of field texts as researchers in the narrative inquiry tradition. This movement from field work and writing field texts to analysis and interpretive acts, and from there to the composition of research text is often a mysterious process to those new to narrative research and is full of challenging nuances to experienced narrative researchers.

Our hope for this book is that it makes transparent our processes of moving from teacher educator field texts to research texts; in each chapter, authors use examples of teacher educator stories of experience to illustrate underlying processes of interpretation and analysis. We draw upon the metaphor of navigating through a system of braided rivers to illustrate and reflect on this process, specifically in the editor dialogues that follow each chapter. Inherent in this text is also the notion of *narrative inquirers in the midst*. We place this notion centrally to connect it to Clandinin and Connelly's conceptualization of a three-dimensional narrative inquiry space with its genesis in Dewey's philosophy of experience and education. The idea of being "in the midst" (Clandinin & Connelly, 2000) also captures for us the tentative, murky, and fluid process of the interpretive acts that mark the movement between field work and writing to meaning-making of the research text. Finally, in the midst says something about the unifying metaphor for this text. We are all narrative inquiry researchers living among and intertwined with others like braided rivers; our traditions pull from diverse perspectives and methods in our goal of exploring and making sense of experience.

As the authors in this text make transparent their interpretive and analytical acts within the three-dimensional inquiry space, we believe their layered stories can provide a means of supporting scholars new to narrative inquiry and more seasoned scholars interested in a deeper examination of the epistemology and ontology involved in collaborative meaning-making. More specifically, this book:

- illustrates interim narrative field texts of identity as teacher educator stories;
- displays "thinking like a narrative inquirer" (Connelly & Clandinin, 2006)
- demonstrates how researchers utilize the commonplaces of temporality, sociality, and place (Clandinin & Connelly, 2000) in analyzing narratives;
- uncovers tension and conceptualizations of narrative research processes; and,
- illuminates meaning and develops connections between narrative understandings of teacher educator identity in relationship to scholarship in teacher education and identity.

As a starting place, teams of authors identified selected field texts. Each chapter features teacher educators/narrative inquirers presenting, unpacking, and deepening understanding and analysis of their narratives through "temporal unfolding" (Connelly & Clandinin, 2006, p. 485) of these stories over a period of two years. Threaded through their processes are grounding notions such as commonalities and layerings, identity-making, burrowing and broadening, vulnerabilities, attention to ethical questions/wonderings, and relational knowing and research.

GUIDING QUESTIONS

The guiding questions below served us well as a map through the development of the book. They are embedded in the existing theoretical backdrop of narrative inquiry, which adds to the empirical nature of this work. With the intent of providing a sense of continuity throughout this work, readers will see dialogue and references to these questions and the theoretical connections in the in-between spaces (editor dialogues) of the chapters. The meaning-making readers will see in these spaces is where the coeditors make use of the metaphor of braided rivers to make visible the layering, tenuous nature of collaborative analysis.

- What does the three-dimensional narrative space mean?
- What does layering commonalities across story plotlines (time, place, contexts, tensions) look like?
- How is meaning found in these layered commonalities?
- How do narrative inquirers create field texts? How do we share them? How do we interpret them?

- How do field texts become research texts?
- How do we create, then analyze our own field texts in order to think of our teacher educator identities?

STORIES THAT UNPACK THE GOALS OF THIS WORK

As narrative inquirers in the midst of our journeys as researchers and teacher educators, we restory a portion of our journeys here, as an invitation for readers to live alongside us – living, telling, reliving, retelling (Clandinin & Connelly, 1994). What resonance, tension, questions, or stories emerge as we enter the past?

Resonance with the Rough

Elaine – In the early stages of visioning this book, I remembered how when I read about methodological nuances of conducting research using a narrative inquiry approach in Clandinin and Connelly's (2000) book, there seemed to be many questions that arose. Some of these questions were eventually sorted out as we worked as researchers on the Bay Street School. I was thinking that among my goals for this book, one was to reflect upon and to write about some of the nuances that became apparent (and other nuances that seemed to become murkier) as we worked with teachers, students, and others on a school landscape. Many of the methodological points addressed the issue of teacher knowledge, and more specifically, developed teacher knowledge. Although my work is based on school and school community research, many of the issues could also refer to other research situations when a researcher is using a narrative inquiry approach.

Another of my goals for this work was to raise questions, and to consider possible ways of addressing questions through analysis of research participant relationships and exploration into our own interpretations. This stance reveals complexities of researcher participant relationships and highlights the role of inquiry in the work of teacher educators. I find this inquiry stance refreshing as well as thought provoking since it moves our thinking beyond what is presented in our writing. This inquiry quality speaks loudly in Vivian Paley's work (1998, 2000) as well as in the Clandinin and Connelly's (2000) work. Finally, I like the idea of a "rough," as opposed to definitive or overly analyzed interpretation of our stories. Early words from one of the chapter authors, M. Shaun Murphy, about the appeal of presenting our field texts in rough form to illustrate ways in which we might begin interpretation, resonated with me.

I really like the idea of the braided rivers (see below), not only because they are so cool to look at from above, but because they highlight the power of the idea of resonance as we respond to the work of others. My memory goes back to Tuesday nights during my doctoral program (our Works in Progress sessions) and to our Foundations of Curriculum classes when we took turns presenting our work, and then responding to the work of our colleagues through written letters. I found it immensely satisfying to have the opportunity to think about the work while listening to the details presented by our colleagues, and then to respond to it deeply in ways that reflected our own interpretation and experiences. The structure provided a framework for learning about the work of others as well as responding to this work in ways that reflected our learning and thinking at that point in time. In January of 2010 as Shaun, Janice, Vicki, and I were preparing for the Narrative, Arts-based Post-Approaches to Social Research (NAPAR) conference, I was struck by how powerful the need was to respond to the work of others through our own experiences. So, I think I see this idea of the connections between parts of the rivers as ways in which we may connect to the work of others. In the process of demonstrating this response process through our writing at the ends of the chapters, we also envisioned this as a means of modeling the process for the readers so that they could also respond to the stories we present with stories of their own.

Tools of Meaning-Making

Vicki – When first invited into the process of thinking through the concept of this book, the experience I planned to share with new narrative researchers was based on my journey moving through the murkiness of uncertainty. As a beginning researcher, my first instinct was to let my field notes speak for themselves. I have good talent at conveying details in my observation notes, and what I wanted to share with readers was contained in the descriptions of the people, places, and interactions in my research sites. However, it was through the process of writing my dissertation that taught me *the process of analysis* is where I make meaning of the experience. The two analysis tools that I came to feel the most comfortable with were the curriculum commonplaces and the narrative dimensions. In fact, I find in my research, writing, and teaching, and thinking about teaching that I naturally and habitually turn to these conceptual tools to help me make meaning of experiences. Because I find these two analysis tools so helpful in my own work, I was pleased by the prospect of sharing these with other narrative researchers. However, As Janice, Shaun, and I began the process of writing, I had a surprise – I found myself learning a new way of making meaning of stories. I absolutely loved the process... it made me think deeply and moved me into thoughts, feelings, memories that I do not often make accessible to others, even to myself. The meaning-making in which I engaged for our chapter involved the laying of experiences against one another, layering and weaving together stories. My surprise was that in the very act of attending to the images, thoughts, and memories that were called forth in response to an initiating story is, in itself, a meaning-making moment. Something in Shaun's story made me travel through my history to find a touchstone experience that answered his. What was my mind looking for? Why did my stories self select the image it did? What were the connections I was making? Had I jumped to my tried and true methods of analysis or fallen into a comfortable and safe way of writing and researching, I may have missed the analysis that my *self* was doing in an autobiographical meaning-making way.

The Value in Raw, Relational, Temporary Spaces

Dixie – In my third year as a teacher educator, I was entangled – "in the midst" – of making sense of the politics and systems involved in higher education. And many of my stories were centered in tension. When invited by Mary Lynn Hamilton and Stefinee Pinnegar to write about my "place" as a teacher educator, stories of tension and bumps on my professional landscape quickly emerged. My unease with some of these stories paralleled the growing unease and negative perception of teacher preparation programs in our country. Here I had just begun my journey on the higher education landscape, and I seemed to be facing the onslaught of my profession – from federal educational policy in America like "Race to the Top" to a growing demand from state policymakers for teacher education program accountability. Since our invitations to write based on the curriculum commonplaces led to the presentations of our writings and collaborations at the NAPAR Conference in January of 2010, my discomfort in sharing my writings lessened when I heard one of the keynote speakers share the message, "*Leave it raw.*" Was my tense narrative of place valuable to someone who may be feeling the onslaught as well? Would other beginning teacher educators be wondering about their places and examining tensions of place and conferring with mentors for vision and ways to sustain themselves? Just as in *Narrative Inquiry* – when Clandinin and Connelly (2000) unpack their own story of "coming to narrative" and of answering the question, "Why narrative?" – by participating in the invitation to write about this tense place, I was choosing "showing" rather than "telling" as to "what narrative inquirers do" (p. 20).

So, our symposium (which began the work on this book) happened at the NAPAR conference in Tempe, Arizona. Besides hearing the other stories of teacher educators involved in the symposium group, I listened to other speakers at the conference, experienced and established narrative researchers in the field of education. My tensions found commonality with the words I heard. I embraced the *"complexities of collaboration, housed in experiences with others,"* from Janet Miller (Keyes, NAPAR Conference notes, 2010). She also gave me the words that described the way Cheryl Craig, my chapter coauthor, led me to explore the notion of "betrayal" within our "place" as teacher educators as it emerged with all its complexities. Because of my collaboration with Cheryl for the symposium, I was exposed to the murky nature of interpreting place. Also noted by Miller, *"a research collaborative embodies relationality, predicated on flows, moves, and challenges"* (Keyes, NAPAR Conference notes, 2010). After hearing the collaborative writings of the other narrative inquirers in our presentation group, I quickly realized that we could connect how the aspects of collaboration embodied relationship throughout what would soon be the chapters of this book. The "flows" and "moves" depicted in the field texts shared by the chapter authors provided unique "challenges" for each researcher.

I also broadened my understandings of laying my stories alongside those of others as Janet helped me make another connection, *"autobiographical educational research disrupts normalized practices"* (Keyes, NAPAR Conference notes, 2010). There is necessity in laying our stories alongside – this process adds to the empirical quality of narrative inquiry and explains why lived experience and why personal, practical knowledge is so central to narrative and the impact narratives can have on the lives and landscapes of educators and their students.

Eliot Eisner, also a keynote speaker at the conference, reminded me of the "tools" narrative inquirers use, ones that note narrative is "always on the move," in *temporary spaces*. This depicts well the work of narrative inquirers and the understanding of *ambiguity, temporality, and relationship*. *"We think through the tools we use"* (Keyes, NAPAR Conference notes, 2010). We can embrace the vulnerable (which is often found in ambiguity or temporary truth, and in the state of not knowing or of formulating new knowledge) through the different "tools" represented in the chapters (i.e., Dixie's tracing, responses from a mentor – making meaning together, writing narratives from other's narratives, using knowledge of the

Introducing Braided Rivers xxiii

complexities and structures of narrative to make meaning as in Cathy and Mary's chapter, finding/thinking about theoretical connections/underpinnings that help with meaning-making, and noting the temporal issues of analysis and interpretation (what makes sense now may not make sense later, and what made sense in the past doesn't make sense now, or I can add what I knew in the past to help me make sense of the present)). How valuable would it be for narrative researchers to read of the "tools" within these chapters in order to find or become aware of their own tools? Hence, the call for readers of this text to enter into the commonplaces with us.

Finally, because of an experience Elaine communicated in a coeditor SKYPE call in the Summer of 2011, we bring forward a metaphor that represents the collective collaboration in these writings, and that effectively displays the movement of field notes or field texts to research texts, and the layering of commonalities within the narratives and the analyses shared in this book. As you view the aerial photograph and read Elaine's narrative of the metaphor below, note how the larger, more powerful, or long-lasting, river feeds the others, while some of the others are smaller or larger and wind through and around one another, moving silt, transferring particles, minerals, and life to each other, or change one another's landscapes.

Braided River Metaphor
I stood in awe on the bridge, listening to the call of the birds while looking into the remaining orange–red glow of the sun as it lowered in the horizon. I could

only see the shadow of the birds as they approached the banks of the river, but knew they were nearby by their distinct, almost deafening, calls as they drew closer.

Each March, when the snow has melted but the weather is still brisk, tens of thousands of the world's Sandhill Cranes stop in the Grand Island and Gibbon area of Nebraska on their migration path to settle for the summer months. The birds, described as magnificent and "somewhat skittish" by laypeople, are a common sight in the fields surrounding these waters during the late afternoons as the sun is beginning to set. Initially not of particular interest to me, I was urged by others to go and have a look, and was then lured in by their very interesting habits. So much about these cranes is fascinating, from their sheer size to their roosting habits and patterns of migration.

Each evening, the cranes return to roost for the night in the shallow, braided rivers of the Platte River. The birds circle the nearby fields, feeding on the corn stalks from the previous season. From a distance, I saw the tan-colored birds bent over in the fields, picking at the corn stalks. At nearly four feet tall, their size impressed me; they were among the largest flying birds I had ever seen. I was also intrigued by their subtle movement away from us as we attempted to get closer for a better look; it seemed that the closer we were able to move toward them, the further they receded into the fields. As we watched the sky darken, the birds moved to the Platte River to settle for the evening.

From ground level, the distinctions between the land and water of the braided rivers are difficult to see, but from above, their formations are much more obvious. The rivers weave together and then separate to form low riverbeds with possibilities for nesting in shallow water between the edges of the river. It is this image of the braided rivers, seen from above as well as from ground level, that we will refer to as we describe the process of exploring, sharing, and then responding to the writing and ideas about the interpretation of field notes written by the teacher educators featured in this book. We present the authors as individual rivers, separate and distinct from other seemingly parallel rivers, whose ideas at times come together and are shared and explored. The rivers then separate again, to join with another river further along. This metaphor of the coming together of ideas, as illustrated by the joining of the rivers, and then the parting of ideas that is illustrated by the separation of the rivers to continue further along the stream, provided an image for the writing and sharing of teacher educator experiences through field texts and then research texts.

INTRODUCING THE CHAPTERS

Openness and Inconclusivity in Interpretation in Narrative Inquiry: Dimensions of the Social/Personal by Stefinee Pinnegar and Mary Lynn Hamilton

The authors, in this chapter, examine the process of narrative analysis within the three-dimensional narrative space from the particular perspective of the personal/social. In uncovering narrative understandings about interpretation and analysis, the authors explore further four insights: (1) in moving field texts to research texts narrative researchers begin in the midst and naturally draw upon interpretive tools from other experiences in meaning-making; (2) as the researchers attend to sociality, looking inward and outward, place and temporality slide naturally, fruitfully and tacitly into developing understandings; (3) in the perpetual motion of moving from internal/external, the researchers found themselves laying narratives alongside one other so that self is inextricably interwoven in the process; and (4) as analysis deepens, ethical issues regarding relationships between teachers, teacher educators, and the duty to unseen children emerge. Examining carefully the experience of engaging in the three-dimensional narrative space, the researchers found that stories live alongside their meaning-making, and often the sense they make of a new story emerges through the provision of a different, new story that repositions through plot, theme, and character the learning at which they arrive. Just as experience never ends and is only bounded for a particular interpretation, story escapes from analysis to assert meanings that remains open to restorying or the reconstruction of new understandings.

Burrowing and Broadening in the Storied Place of Teacher Education by Dixie Keyes and Cheryl Craig

As Cheryl lays her stories of place (in higher education as a teacher educator) alongside Dixie's traced stories of place, they find themselves using several interpretive tools to explore the question, "What sustains us as teacher educators?" Dixie begins with "tracing" moments and stories of place, attending to the temporal nature of meaning-making. Cheryl initially "burrows" into the puzzle, then "broadens" her experiences to contemporary tensions, looking inward and outward to uncover the constant motion in stories of place. Cheryl deepens the dialogue as she makes her professional knowledge landscape more visible, bringing *sacred stories, stories of gender, stories of hierarchy, stories of power*, and *stories of race* forward, exploring how these stories are held in tension with one another, visible to some but only faintly discernible to others. The authors ponder the questions: what happens when the *small stories* educators are living in place become so far removed from authorized *meta-narratives* also under way in place? And, how can we remain wakeful to the many *story constellations* of others that revolve around us?

Attending to the Temporal Dimension of Narrative Inquiry into Teacher Educator Identities by M. Shaun Murphy, Vicki Ross, and Janice Huber

The authors focus, first, on the relational nature of narrative inquiry and ways in which they became entangled in one another's knowing, and lives, through sharing stories. This beginning shapes the process as Shaun shares a story, followed by storied responses from Janice, and Vicki. The narrative commonplace of temporality (Connelly & Clandinin, 2006) is strongly foregrounded in this relational process. The storytelling and response draws forward past narratives to respond to one another, as the authors simultaneously inquire into the shaping influence of these past experiences in the present "stories we live by" (Connelly & Clandinin, 1999) as teacher educators. The storied responses to one another's stories become layered one upon another. Evident to the authors was that they were also writing of sociality and place in their narratives. They were situated as narrative inquirers and teacher educators looking inward and outward as they took moments of personal significance and situated them in the context of social significance. Staying attentive to the commonplace of temporality helped them stay wakeful to how the past and future are understood in the context of the present.

Exploring Chronotopic Shifts between Known and Unknown in our Teacher Educator Identity Narratives by Mary Rice and Cathy Coulter

In this chapter, the authors explore their own teacher educator identity narratives by making visible the analytical use of chronotope, a tool from Bakhtin's literature theory. Chronotope functions as a conceptual research tool for teacher identity plotlines when interfaced with other appropriate programs of research. The authors generated their methods alongside a review of literature in several interlocking pieces. One set of pieces involves reviewing research on teacher educator identity. In set, they grew their analysis by placing it alongside understandings about identity in general. Juxtaposing their stories against a narrative inquiry research base and a literary tool enabled them to find multilayered meanings in their stories.

Cross-Cultural Interpretation of Field Texts by Candace Schlein and Elaine Chan

In this chapter, the authors explore some of the nuances of interpreting field texts while taking into consideration the potential influence of the cultural, racial, religious, ethnic, or linguistic backgrounds of the researchers and their participants in shaping the interpretation of field texts. In particular, they present and examine field texts that shed light on key curricular experiences, spaces, and silences. The authors refer to Clandinin and Connelly's (2000) notion of the three-dimensional narrative inquiry space to explore and deliberate over ways in which culture may contribute to interpretation of field texts while also intersecting dimensions of time, space, and sociality. They also raise issues of participant vulnerability and ethics in participant relationships, as well as "investment of self in the inquiry" (Connelly & Clandinin, 2006).

REFERENCES

Clandinin, D. J., & Connelly, F. M. (1994). Personal experience methods. In N. K. Denzin & Y. S. Lincoln (Eds.), *Handbook of qualitative research* (pp. 413–427). Thousand Oaks, CA: Sage.

Clandinin, D. J., & Connelly, F. M. (2000). *Narrative inquiry: Experience and story in qualitative research*. San Francisco, CA: Jossey-Bass.

Connelly, F. M., & Clandinin, D. J. (Eds.). (1999). *Shaping a professional identity: Stories of educational practice*. New York, NY: Teachers College Press.

Connelly, F. M., & Clandinin, D. J. (2006). Narrative inquiry. In J. Green, G. Camilli & P. Elmore (Eds.), *Handbook of complementary methods in educational research* (pp. 477–489). Washington, DC: American Educational Research Association.

Paley, V. (1998). *The girl with the brown crayon: How children use stories to shape their lives*. Cambridge, MA: Harvard University Press.

Paley, V. (2000). *White teacher*. Cambridge, MA: Harvard University Press.

CHAPTER ONE

OPENNESS AND INCONCLUSIVITY IN INTERPRETATION IN NARRATIVE INQUIRY: DIMENSIONS OF THE SOCIAL/PERSONAL

Stefinee Pinnegar and Mary Lynn Hamilton

ABSTRACT

Purpose – *In this chapter, we examine the influence of the commonplace of sociality within narrative inquiry during the process of interpretation and meaning-making. Our project was multivisioned because we were interested in what we learned about the methodology of narrative inquiry within the context of a phenomenon for inquiry (Clandinin & Connelly, 2000), which for this study was our identity as teacher educators (Bullough, 2005).*

Approach – *Using narrative inquiry, we interrogate our interpretive processes privileging the commonplace of sociality in examining stories of our identity as teacher educators from our own experience as teacher educators.*

Findings – *In our inquiry into interpretation from the orientation of the narrative commonplace of the social, four points of understanding* emerged: *(1) interpretation within the methodology of narrative inquiry is living and interpretation exists in the midst; (2) all three dimensions of the narrative inquiry space are always part of the process regardless of the commonplace under consideration; (3) if we look inward/outward in the process of interpretation, it always leads us back to the relational; and (4) when we deepen the analytic process, ethical issues, and therefore renewed grappling with our identity, emerge.*

Research implications – *Narrative inquiry at every phase – design, data collection, analysis, and representation – is a form of living and analysis and interpretation. As well, representation must allow space for the holistic and organic quality that this form of inquiry demands in the development and communication of ideas.*

Value – *The study points to the ways in which research on humans' action and interaction returns to the relational and ethical even when that is not the focus of the research. Further, our response to narrative inquiry is not always analysis but often turns to story instead.*

Keywords: Teacher education; teacher educator; narrative analysis; field text; ethical

> For us, doing narrative inquiry is a form of living. Living in its most general sense, is unbounded. The structures, seen and unseen, that do constrain our lives when noticed can always be imagined to be otherwise, to be more open, to have alternative possibilities. This very notion is embedded in the area of retelling stories and reliving lives. Our narrative inquiry intention is to capture as much as possible this openness of experience. (Clandinin & Connelly, 2000, p. r89)

We sit together at a table in Edmonton, breathing in and out – indeed living. A pleasant breeze blows through the window and we take up the task of exploring the experience of engaging in narrative analysis from the perspective of the social/personal. Mary Lynn begins to read aloud the quote with which we open this chapter, "For us, narrative inquiry is a form of living." In that moment, Stefinee thinks, "Yes! What a great way to begin. We do think narrative inquiry is a form of living." But Mary Lynn continues reading and Stefinee realizes, "Oh! this is a quote from Clandinin and Connelly, not something we said." Stefinee laughs and shares her misunderstanding, and we are simultaneously struck by the ways in which the misunderstanding captures the notions of inquiry and interpretation revealed in the quote.

Narrative inquiry is a form of living; and as a form of living, its boundaries are permeable and as we inquire, multiple forms of knowledge – formal, informal, tacit – flow within our inquiry and inform us as we attempt to analyze experiences that we have identified as in some way relating to the phenomenon we are studying. The quote we begin with, of itself, brings forward that quality. We have experience with the whole of this text, and while we point to only this quote in our minds, other quotes from the book press into our consciousness. We have had experiences and interactions with the authors of the text, and the text prompts to our memories some of these experiences. In addition, specific places in the text interject into our interpretive processes. Further, just as Stefinee imagined the text to be one of her and Mary Lynn's composing, when we analyze narratives we can imagine stories to be different from how they actually occur. These differences then push into our interpretation of the narratives we analyze so that what is not present as well as what is present becomes part of the analysis because narrative inquiry as a living form opens these possibilities. One of the difficulties of engaging then in data analysis or interpretation within the framework of narrative inquiry is just this point – narrative inquiry as a research methodology is a form of living. Thus, wherever one stands within a narrative inquiry project one is always in the midst of living it. As Leitch (1986) argues, we live our lives in middles and beginnings, and ends emerge from middles when we talk about our experience and tell and retell stories of our lives.

In living our lives, structures both seen and unseen may constrain us, but in inquiring into our experience – since it is a form of living – the interpretive processes can allow us to make visible the constraints and potentially free us from them. It is also as the Clandinin and Connelly quote suggests, plotlines and interactions can be imagined as having alternative possibilities to the extent that our analysis and our representation of it invite those reading the work to imagine endings as beginning, middles as endings, and beginnings and endings as well as alternatives to the beginnings, middles, and endings presented. As narrative inquirers, we invite researchers to not only understand the current contexts and constraints in lived experiences but also rethink the contexts and constraints and think of new ways to be in relationship in their own experiences related to the phenomenon of the inquiry. It is in interpretation of experience where story resides and the potential for telling, retelling, and reliving emerge.

The subtitle of Clandinin and Connelly's (2000) methodology book, *Narrative Inquiry: Experience and Story in Qualitative Research*, captures the living quality of this methodology. We inquire into our experience by making it story, and our stories are made meaningful because of our experiences. They argue that in constructing and telling a story of our experience – communicating the meaning we are making of it – we open the opportunity for retelling that narrative and potentially reliving it. In analysis, we lay stories of our scholarly study or of our past experiences alongside our work to help us make meaning of the analysis and to explain the meanings we are making or invite ourselves or others to think how things might be other than they are.

In the moments of analysis and interpretation, as Clandinin and Connelly (2000) indicate, our past stories become open for retelling–reliving–reinterpretation. Others can draw these stories and the possibilities they open for living forward into their lives and experiences. As we make meaning of our experiences, meanings shift or are deepened since what appears settled and done becomes open again and again.

If narrative inquiry is a form of living and the meanings we are trying to understand emerge as we make sense of the experiences we inquire into, then the inquiry space, as we have noted, is always ambiguous and open, allowing for meaning-making to materialize as memories, tensions, constraints – both imagined and real – bump against each other and coalesce as points of insight and understanding. These insights and understandings we arrive at in the course of our inquiry lead us to determine where in the research text we want to invite readers to reimagine the constraints experienced by those involved in the story and take up the possibility that the story might or could end or be lived differently and that we might in our own interactions with schools, teachers, children engage in ways that open new possibility.

Identification of the points of constraint and the insights attached to them are the work of interpretation. Systematic processes of data collection and interpretation can enable us to be more rigorous in our explorations of meaning. The systematic process proposed by Clandinin and Connelly (2000) is the use of the three-dimensional narrative space. By using the three commonplaces of time, place, and personal/social, we can become wakeful to how participants, events, and objects are "placed at a particular moment, temporally, spatially and in terms of the personal and social" (Clandinin & Connelly, 2000, p. 89) and we can imagine how there might be other possibilities. In articulating how to engage in analysis within narrative inquiry, Clandinin and Connelly (2000) propose the use of the three-dimensional narrative space whose commonplaces or dimensions include, time, place, and the social/personal.

COMMONPLACE OF TIME

In narrative inquiry, the "events under study are always in temporal transition" (Connelly & Clandinin, 2006, p. 479). This means that narrative inquirers play with the boundary of time not only imagining that things might have occurred in a different order, but also reimagining the influence of the chronology of experience on the meaning made. Experience is always characterized by having a past, present, and a future or the commonplace of time. When we engage in interpreting data, whatever event we have chosen to label as "the beginning" of a narrative is the point from which we choose to begin. However, usually we are not too far into the story when we find ourselves drawing past experiences or details forward that occurred chronologically earlier or even later (perhaps even beyond the end point of the story) in order to make clearer or provide evidence for the meaning we are making. In analysis from this orientation, we open the recorded experience to potential and possibility. We embrace Bakhtin's (1981) zone of maximal contact – the zone of inconclusivity. For Bakhtin, this is the point at which we bring forward a past in connection with a present and reimagine possible and multiple futures rather than a certain one. He argues that as these points in time coalesce, our understanding in the present allows us to reconceive of the past and reimagine the future and in this way the past, present, and future are all altered.

During the analysis of an event in order to open interpretation and possibility, we deliberately position the narrative in this zone of inconclusivity making the boundaries of time permeable. We do this by intentionally shifting across the dimension – remembering past experience (how we were, what we thought things meant, and what that means for now), anticipating where this current plotline is heading (projecting our past or current understandings into the future), and thinking of our response in terms of what did or does constrain us. In inquiring into our experience, this shifting across the dimensions of time embedded in the narrative reveals both our understandings and misunderstandings of the story. Intentionally making the time boundary permeable opens new ways of thinking and understanding our experience allowing us to rethink where the humans, events, conditions, and contexts of this experience might have been or potentially could be different than it is. This intentional shifting can free us from limitations and constraints on our thinking about experience and opens for consideration boundaries and concepts that in the original living or even telling of the experience we represented as static, permanent, or unalterable.

Connelly and Clandinin suggest that when we begin systematically exploring experience by moving forward and backward along the dimension of time, our inquiry into the story and our interpretation of it are changed. We inquire differently into our experiences because bringing past, present, and future opens static, time-imposed boundaries, and this shifting can reveal constraints as well as allow us to inquire into them.

In making meaning of narratives, experiences in interpretation that lead us to alter time and ultimately rearrange chronology, either in our explorations or in interpretations of narratives, can open and reopen spaces and disrupt traditional narrative structures, constraints, and plotlines allowing for reimaginings.

COMMONPLACE OF PLACE

The history, culture, constraints, and meanings that permeate an experience shape the story we tell of the experience. Any narrative inquiry, because it engages and explores experience, is situated – "events take place somewhere" (Connelly & Clandinin, 2006, p. 481). The inquiry and the stories that emerge from it have topological and physical boundaries and features (Connelly & Clandinin, 2006). We make meaning by considering the ways in which contexts and place shape experience and stories. We deepen our understanding, when we make the constraints permeable and imagine how the experience might have been different if the boundaries might have been more open or how a context need not restrict what happens. As we uncover the constraints that place and situatedness contribute to the meaning of a story, we open and reopen these boundaries and imagine potential differences in the beginnings, endings, and possible futures. We also consider how context shapes relationships, actions, and experience and how different circumstances, organizational structures, cultural norms, policies, and landscapes might have led to different plotlines being shaped on this landscape or enacted in this place.

COMMONPLACE OF SOCIALITY

In the three-dimensional inquiry space, sociality includes the social elements and the personal elements and represents the personal conditions and the social conditions. The personal conditions include feelings, hopes, desires, esthetic reactions, and moral dispositions of the person, along with his or her social environment including the surrounding factors and forces, people and otherwise, within that person's context (Connelly & Clandinin, 2006).

This commonplace, which asks that we look inward and move outward (Connelly & Clandinin, 2006), examines the social relationships and interaction within a story, the shared understandings of how people interact in these settings and the way in which people feel about what unfolds. As we work to understand meaning-making in an experience, we consider the social relationships and interactions that occur among people in the experience. We consider what is felt and what is said and unsaid in the conversational exchanges, the verbal and nonverbal communication, and the ways in which people position each other and are positioned (both in terms of the person-to-person interchanges as well as the social and cultural norms of the situation and community). We examine the assumptions that are implicit in these interactions both for individuals and for cultures and communities. We consider the issues of status and power and hierarchies among people individually as well as socially and within and across cultures.

As we took up this investigation into how the social/personal dimension of the three-dimensional narrative space influences interpretation during inquiry, we soon realized that during analysis into a narrative, even though the interpretation might be oriented toward one commonplace or another (time, place, social/personal), the other two would always be part of the interpretive process. Shifting time or reconsidering place both reveal and open constraints so that we might consider the status, power, boundaries, feelings, attitudes, and interactions in relationships to be different than they are.

FOCUS OF THE INQUIRY

For this chapter, we are interested in the role of the commonplace of sociality in the process of interpretation and meaning-making within narrative inquiry. Thus, just as in any narrative inquiry our project was multivisioned; we were interested in what we could learn about the methodology of narrative inquiry within the context of a phenomenon for inquiry (Clandinin & Connelly, 2000). We decided for this study to focus on our sense of identity as teacher educators (Bullough, 2005) as the phenomenon we would explore.

IDENTIFYING DATA FOR THE STUDY

We realize that stories are layered within a whole life. The boundaries between daily life and professional life are permeable and yet bump constantly against each other. In the bumping, they remind us of our privilege and our constraints. As teacher educators and academics, we experience lives in which we simultaneously live out many plotlines, such as faculty member, colleague, friend, mother, wife, person, teacher, teacher educator, and teacher educator researcher. While the stories we tell may highlight only one of these plotlines, in our experience the others are ever present and can therefore constrain or advantage us. Tensions emerge when the plotlines exist in competition or conflict with each other and we find ourselves simultaneously enacting two or more roles. Indeed, our personal and familial obligations can push against obligations we have as teacher educators as we struggle to meet the needs of preservice teachers or faculty members. The tensions that emerge as we attempt to enact our obligations, responsibilities, and duties lead us to notice potentialities and constraints. These tensions and attendant understandings are connected to the development of identity as teacher educators, and this is the focus of our inquiry about interpretation of stories of being teacher educators from the perspective of the commonplace of the social/personal.

As we (Mary Lynn and Stefinee) took up this study, we realized we had written many studies of ourselves as teacher educators, and so we determined to use for the study a story from earlier published accounts. We each agreed to examine our published articles and identify a story of our *self* as a teacher educator. In this conversation, Stefinee suggested several stories from each of our past publications, and as the conversation ended Stefinee had in her mind a story of Mary Lynn's that she sought to find a resonant story for. However, as Stefinee reviewed her published pieces, she had a difficult time identifying a story that she felt was really a story of herself as a teacher educator and that also resonated with Mary Lynn's story.

One day as she sat in her office working with a research assistant who was also a preservice teacher, an experience emerged. She wrote the story and then she sent it to the preservice teacher. She asked the preservice teacher if she might use the story for this work. The preservice teacher amended the story adding some details and questioning others. They then met together and negotiated the final text that appears in this account. Stefinee then sent the story to Mary Lynn. After reading Stefinee's story, Mary Lynn identified a story from a published piece. Interestingly, the story Mary Lynn identified was the story with which Stefinee had sought a piece to resonate.

Stefinee's Story

> It was Friday morning at 8 am. My office window provides a frame for a panoramic view of mountains that surround the university campus on three sides. My undergraduate research assistant sits at a table next to me. She has been working on a literature review

focused on the topic of preservice teachers' development as teachers of English Language Learners (ELLs). We have both been working quietly for a moment or two. I'm answering e-mail and the student is pulling out her article summaries. As she hands them to me, I put my e-mail aside for later and skim the two page summaries she has produced. She has done a good job on the summaries. I finish reading them and ask her about the progress she has made in reading the book that focuses on teaching ELLs. She pulls up her notes and summarizes the sections she has read, and as usual, raises questions that are coming from her reading or notes the places where she thinks the arguments made by the author are less than strong. It is a lively discussion. As she finishes with her review of her reading in the book, I ask her, "What did you find interesting about the articles you read this week?"

She begins by saying, "Well, I think I understand the article quite well. Do you want me to just talk about what I understand from the article or can I talk about how I feel about it?"

Ironically, since I'm quite intense about research findings myself, I am caught off-guard by her question wondering what there was to feel about these articles which were for the most part reviews of research on content-based teaching and educating the beliefs and attitudes of preservice teachers regarding teaching culturally and linguistically diverse students. I do want to know what she feels about her reading, so I invite her to continue.

She says, "It made me furious. The author began by saying that the overwhelming majority of preservice teachers are White, female, middle to upper-middle class, Christian women ... well that describes me. Then she just slams us. She reviews article after article that reports that we are racist and that we will not meet the needs or be good at educating culturally and linguistically diverse students. I come from a city known to be racially and ethnically diverse with a wide range of class differences. I went to public schools there. Many of my friends came from backgrounds that were culturally different from mine. I don't think I have racist beliefs. I think my friends would – well my friends have said that I was not racist and that I am a good friend. She argues that as a teacher I will reproduce the same racist schools that I was educated in. She does make the statement once or twice that not all students are like this but then she just slams us again and again. She thinks she's hidden it, but she's talking about me and she asserts over and over again that I am deficit. I feel like the charges she is making about me being a racist and likely to enact racist practices against my students could just as easily be applied to her.

She doesn't know me. She doesn't know the other preservice teachers I take classes with. She just lumps me in with everyone. Also, these are her preservice teachers – her own students she is talking about. How does she think they will feel about her when they read what she has written about them."

"She's just reporting the research." I try to temporize.

"I can understand that, but I can tell she didn't think preservice teachers would ever read this article and so she just slams us. She just labels all preservice teachers who are White, Christian, middle-class females as difficult and as unable to not be prejudiced toward their students. I think we have to be fair to everyone and we should hold all of our students to high standards."

Mary Lynn's Story

In order for this description to have the proper impact you have to imagine the scene. Here we are, my class and I, in an oversized room with too many school desks. It is the end of the football season; we are playing our serious rivals. My students mostly look like Barbie and Ken dolls ... . So there they are, arriving in class precisely on time. In the front of the room is their teacher. Me, I look like I have studied the conservative republic book of dress ... . Today is our first whole group meeting in weeks ... . I begin by asking if anyone has any management miracles from their observations ... . Quickly the issues turn to human dignity ... just as quickly I begin to talk about revolution in the schools. But, I did not begin the discussion before I, unconsciously, walked over and closed the classroom door ... you would have been proud. There I was professing revolution. Their little eyes wide; there was a lot of whispering. I used my favorite quote from the Mohawks in Quebec ... today is a good day to die ... I asked them to consider the issues for which they were willing to take a stand. They were mesmerized. I personally, was scared. (Arizona Group, 1994, November 14, p. 78)

Examining Interpretation

When Mary Lynn begins to apply the social/personal dimension, she is immediately struck by how although she constructed this research text and it has actually been a long time since she participated in this experience, the story resonates with her. It calls forth memories of other late fall and early spring days when she has invited her students into revolution and challenged them about what they are willing to die for. This sense of time collapsing wherein similar events across many years flood her memory making her aware of the permeability of the dimension of time and the way in which when an event is written down and published, time somehow remains fluid. As she experiences this sense of fluidity of time, she recognizes that this story represents only a fragment of her experience, however the whole of the experience as well as the echoes of other experiences is still in her mind as she takes up interpretation. Thus, she reminds us that in analysis, we often lay stories of our past experiences alongside our work to help us make meaning of the analysis or to explain the meanings we are making. In that moment, our past stories become open for retelling and reinterpretation and our experiences as well as their meanings shift or are deepened since what appears settled and done is now open. This brings forward the quote with which we began this chapter, and we remember that narrative inquiry is a form of living.

In her story, Stefinee set the scene by describing the setting, a routine pattern of a meeting she's having with a student. She's reading e-mail and the student prepares to report on her work. Against this routine, which the narrative implies, Stefinee and her student have repeated many times and in which they have rather flat roles, this time, in this middle, the student disrupts the nonemotional tone of the meeting and opens new learning – pulling in her past experience as evidence and her own feelings as text. As the student turns inward, revealing her feeling, she also questions assumptions frequently asserted in the research literature about preservice teachers. Her response leads us to wonder about the accuracy of the assertions we make about the racism of preservice teachers. We recognize the constraints we, as teacher educators, may be placing on preservice teachers' learning and potential to learn, and our analysis here causes us to wonder about the research landscape if preservice teachers actually have taken up plotlines of culturally sensitive pedagogy rather than hegemony.

As we take up a field text, memories of the days before and the days after or other memories the event prompted, we read the outward interactions and relations and are caught as well by the inward and internal relationships revealed in the text. This is made visible in Mary Lynn's story where, in telling her story, she actually orchestrates that by pulling us in as characters when she says:

> In order for this description to have the proper impact you have to imagine the scene. Here we are, arriving in class precisely on time. In the front of the room is their teacher. Me. I look like I have studied the conservative republican book of dress ... Today is our first whole group meeting in weeks ... I begin by asking if anyone has any management miracles from their observations.

As readers, we notice we are standing in the midst of both Stefinee's and Mary Lynn's stories not only seeing them through their eyes but also seeing through our own. In Mary Lynn's story, she has invited the reader (listener) to stand next to the writer. The writer as the narrative inquirer is telling and interpreting the story and inviting us as readers to observe by placing us as an actor in the story. Phrases like "conservative republican school of dress" provide images of what she looks like, but given our own experience some may pause at that phrase, wondering over what it might mean depending on our experience and understanding.

In the three dimensions of the inquiry space, sociality includes the social elements and what forms the individual context. This commonplace, which asks that we look inward and move outward (Connelly & Clandinin, 2006), examines the social relationships and interaction in a story.

In Mary Lynn's story we see this in her references to "the last football of the season," the description of her students as "Barbie and Ken dolls," and herself in "conservative republican dress." Then she strips off the stereotypic with the phrase, "But, I did not begin the discussion before I, unconsciously, walked over and closed the classroom door ... ." Suddenly her relationship with her students changed as they become "wide-eyed" and "whisper." At this point she moves from the outward to the inward, "I was scared."

We can see this more straightforwardly in Stefinee's story, because the student puts this dichotomy forward when she says, "Do you want me to just talk about what I understand from the article or can I talk about how I feel about it?" Here, we have the student reporting well-known and accepted research findings and then laying her own feelings of betrayal and anger alongside those findings by inserting the personal perspective of the preservice teacher – a different one from that found in the article being reviewed. Her question and her response to it ultimately insert relationships and raise questions about the obligations we have in our public and private relationships with our students. Her response calls forth tensions between work as teacher educators, as researchers, and as teachers. We find ourselves standing in a different relationship to the moral assertions we often make about the hegemonic and institutional racism of teachers both inservice and preservice.

This commonplace allows us to distinguish our studies from highly personal studies that focus mostly on a person's thoughts and feelings and to distinguish our narrative inquiry from personal stories since the personal internal meaning making brings depth to the social and outward relationships, while the social and outward meaning making confronts and deepens the inward reflection and personal meaning. In narrative inquiry, analysis situates us (readers and inquirers) in the midst and requires that we attend to and make sense of both (Connelly & Clandinin, 2006).

In every aspect of the analysis process including selecting texts for representation of our ideas and learning, each of the three dimensions is important and each contributes to the development of empirically grounded understandings that emerge from the data. In our analytic process, all of the three commonplaces are present in any analysis.

In Stefinee's story, she creates a sense of space that partitions off the story being analyzed by describing her office space in a way that uses the description of the landscape to mark the space as separate from life. In making the space separate, she also places it outside of normal reckonings of time. We have a sense of her being in a space of insight and reflection without a sense of past, present, or future.

Mary Lynn does a similar thing in her narrative because after telling readers how to position themselves in her classroom space and what they will see there, she shuts the door. She writes:

> There I was professing revolution. Their little eyes were wide. There was a lot of whispering. I used my favorite quote from the Mohawks in Quebec. "Today is a good day to die." I asked them to consider the issues for which they were willing to take a stand.

In this act, Mary Lynn marks this space as separate from the out-of-classroom spaces of Stefinee's university, and like Stefinee, she also marks this space as outside of time. In this act, Mary Lynn marks this as a zone of inconclusivity by bringing events from disparate times together in this space and simultaneously asking students to bring in their past, present, and what they think are their future ways of being and reconsider them – what will they ... what are they willing to die for?

The three-dimensional space wherein analysis occurs in narrative inquiry always takes into account not just the commonplace being examined, but in the examination itself, the other two commonplaces are always there. As we "slide" among the dimensions, tensions around the relational and obligations to the ethical will surface.

When Stefinee returns to her story, she is struck by this preservice teacher's sense that she has a history of friends and relationships with culturally diverse students, and in her mind is an echo that Mary Lynn's story is probably populated with similar kinds of students. Stefinee has a sense of this preservice teacher as a kind person. From our conversations with other teacher educators and preservice teachers, we know that the response of Stefinee's student is not atypical when teacher educators discuss issues of racism and culturally responsive teaching. But we wonder about the accuracy of the statement that we cannot get beyond the institutional grip laid on our mind. Will we always be trapped in false consciousness no matter how we struggle? That is an uncomfortable thought for us as white women; must we (both us and our students) be racist no matter our desire to teach all students well? We leave this for another day.

But as we take up analysis and find that life experiences sit at the edge of our consciousness as we interpret and analyze the narrative under consideration, we see how quickly our analysis moves from consideration of the narrative elements and the three-dimensional narrative space to considerations of relationship and then to ethical questions.

In this example as teacher educators, we feel tension in the relational obligations we have to our own students and those we have to the students they will teach. As we engage in analysis, echoes of past learning and experience interrupt our process. We are reminded of a discourse in teacher education that has troubled us since graduate school. We think of the ways in which we talk about teachers – our former students – as deficit, as less, as incapable and incompetent. Did we offend them so deeply when they were our students that they could not hear what we were teaching? Were our teachings about methods so alien and undoable in the settings they participate in that they could not hear the ways in which, like in Mary Lynn's story, we were inviting them into revolution, inviting them to determine what values they would live by in their practice? Is our teaching and our dismissive tone about how teachers teach part of the reason teachers consistently represent us as an "ivory tower" to preservice teachers when they are in field work settings or ignore what we try to teach in inservice work?

We are reminded how as graduate students we read the research on teacher learning and so often the researchers were heroes who uncovered the secret unknown reality of the truth about the inappropriate, hegemonic, limited teaching of classroom teachers. In that moment we were invited to read ourselves as that deficit teacher or to separate ourselves as a different species and cross over a delicate bridge where we could stand with our professors as superior in this new knowledge and be critical of all other teachers as we denied our being as teachers and took up a singular identity as researcher.

Ultimately the questions that most resonate for us in this examination of interpretation of stories of our teacher educator identity and the process of interpretation from the perspective of the commonplace of the social are: "What duty do I have to my students and their students?" and "What duty do my students have toward their future students and to me?" As we engage in this line of thinking, we realize there is something about the word "duty" that calls forth feelings of responsibility and a desire to serve others.

DISCUSSION

In this chapter, we focused on the narrative dimension of the social/personal to explore narrative understandings about analysis. In our inquiry into inquiry within the narrative commonplace of the social we uncovered four points: (1) Like all of the process of narrative inquiry, interpretation is living and exists in the midst; (2) all elements of the three-dimensional narrative space are always part of interpretation; (3) our looking inward/outward in the process of interpretation always leads us back to the relational; and (4) as we deepen our analysis, ethical issues emerge.

In the Midst

When moving from field text to research text, we begin in the midst and bring interpretive tools honed from our experience as meaning makers. Our histories with experience in interpretation across our lives shows up as we engage in analysis because as Clandinin & Connelly (2000) suggest we "... slide back and forth between records of experience under study and records of oneself as researcher experiencing the experience" (p. 87) both in the analysis and in the research texts that emerge.

Stefinee's history in literature and literary analysis shows up when she frames the story she is telling and the ways in which she uses literary criticism (e.g., Bal, 1997; Bakhtin, 1981) in framing and interpreting the narratives. One example is when she articulates the ways in which Mary Lynn simultaneously plays the role of narrator, character, and actor in her story and the way in which she invites the reader to stand in one of these roles.

Mary Lynn's academic preparation in working with and developing understanding of cultural models, historical interpretation, and meaning making are there and evident in the language and the structure of the text. In her analysis, it is there when she raises questions about or identifies critical features and meanings regarding issues of social justice, political action, or cultural imagery.

Simultaneity of the Commonplaces

While we attend to sociality, looking inward and outward, place and temporality are always a part of our process. As example after example of our experience in interpretation demonstrate, the commonplaces of the temporal and space are ever present in our analysis that attempted to proceed from the perspective of the commonplace of the social.

Sometimes implicit in narrative analysis of texts as presented in a research article suggest that we can analyze narratives using a single lens or coding system, but careful consideration of narratives and attempts to uncover the meaning in them always have a holistic quality because stories always contain within them temporality, context, and the personal/social dimension. These exist not in pieces but holistically and simultaneously, and as a result, they influence our meaning-making. For when we come to the act of interpretation, we cannot completely deny our emotions, feelings, and understandings as human beings from our understandings as researchers. Just as our story of data collection for this project indicated, when we craft a story or select a narrative we do so not only because it exemplifies the understandings we are arriving at but also because it resonates with us. In our selection of a particular story to put forward as example or to delve deeper into, we may never either question our choice in this way or completely understand the entire source of that resonance.

Emergence of the Relational

When we engage in interpretation in narrative inquiry we engage in a perpetual motion of looking internally/externally. In this motion, what we know from theory and what we know from practice become entangled. We choose in our lives to act in a particular way because we have read research that suggests "warm demanders" get better responses from their students. Thus, while some might label this as an external aspect of the commonplace of the social, it has – because we have taken it up as part of our internal guidelines for action and within our private reflection – become internal. Notice, as well, that this internal guideline taken from research has been taken up because we seek to have particular kinds of relationship with those we have responsibilities for. Thus, we notice that the perpetual motion of living in the midst and our ongoing interpretation of our experience lead us to lay narratives alongside each other from current and past experiences, and in this process, relationship becomes essential. In the act of interpretation within narrative inquiry, the self cannot be subtracted from this process and the process always turns toward relationship and the relational.

Surfacing of Ethical Issues in Interpretation

As we deepen our analysis, ethical issues emerge regarding relationships between teachers, teacher educators, and the duty to unseen children. During the past year, Stefinee has been reading a lot of the literature on educating teachers to work with immigrant populations. As she reads articles such as the one included in her narrative, she finds herself tracking both the understandings being promoted about the findings of such research for the conversation of teacher education research and the emotional response she is having as a teacher educator. These two lay in tension with each other, and her attention fairly rapidly moves toward ethical relationships. At the end of her own story, she finds herself wondering the following: "Is there no other way? How can we teach students to be better teachers when we feel they are deficit? Will all of these teachers actually enact racist and hegemonic practices?"

Ending or Beginning/Analysis or Response

One of the realities of narrative inquiry is that often once we engage in the act of interpreting a narrative, our response is not always analysis; instead we find ourselves producing another story. This was Mary Lynn's experience, and we end with the narrative that resulted from a narrative inquiry into stories of teacher educator identity and interpretation from the dimension of the social:

> Stefinee's story raises so many memories and issues for me. I read through it several times, each time boring deeper into the text, the context, and the subtext. First, like Stefinee, I try to situate myself within the context. I remind myself that consciousness in writing and thinking and being offers a researcher strength while doing the heavy lifting of analysis and interpretation. Green. I sit in my warm green room, the color of avocado and spring, in my rocker, facing the window. A hawk sits low on the fence selecting from the bird menu du jour. The wind blows slightly, ruffling its feathers and the potential meals just hop and flit around with no worries. Mostly there are sparrows, finches and wrens around, with a glint of color from the robins and the cardinals and blue jays.
>
> All the birds seem focused on food; some of them don't realize that they, themselves, are the potential meal. I feel calmly anxious as the scene unfolds. I think; I watch; I watch; I think. Against the green of the room I see brown and leftover fall red and orange on the ground below the trees. Like children, the trees have dropped their clothes and the mother-wind has not picked up after them.
>
> I take a deep breath and focus inwardly. With the intake of air, I recognize similarities between my life as a teacher educator and the backyard drama. As if to sharpen the connections, Spot, a neighbor's black cat, enters the scene like a speeding bullet sending the birds scattering and filling the air with an epithet-ladened screech from the hawk. No being got a meal in that moment, but Spot claimed scene-dominance. The scene is familiar to me, and in some ways I know the potential predators that might show up and I know where the pitfalls are. In trying to prepare students for the pitfalls, I wonder if I make it easier for predators to pounce on students who think they already know.
>
> Academia and the life of a teacher educator in the U.S., or at least in Kansas, has the same sort of unpredictability, the predators in waiting, the prancing hoppers and the sleek Spots, and over the years I have learned that no one holds the same position long.

REFERENCES

Arizona Group. (1994). Letters from beginners: Negotiating the transition from graduate student to assistant professor. *The Journal, 8*(2), 71–82.

Bakhtin, M. (1981). *The dialogic imagination: Four essays.* Austin, TX: University of Texas Press.

Bal, M. (1997). *Narratology: Introduction to the theory of narrative* (2nd ed). Toronto, CA: University of Toronto Press.
Bullough, R. V., Jr. (2005). The quest for identity in teaching and teacher education. In G. Hoban (Ed.), *The missing links in teacher education design: Developing a conceptual framework* (pp. 237–258). Netherlands: Springer.
Clandinin, D. J., & Connelly, F. M. (2000). *Narrative inquiry: Experience and story in qualitative research*. San Francisco, CA: Jossey-Bass.
Connelly, F. M., & Clandinin, D. J. (2006). Narrative inquiry. In J. L. Green, G. Camilli & P. Elmore (Eds.), *Handbook of complementary methods in education research* (3rd ed., pp. 477–487). Mahwah, NJ: Lawrence Erlbaum.
Leitch, T. M. (1986). *What stories are: Narrative theory and interpretation*. University Park, TX: The Pennsylvania State University.

CHAPTER ONE BRAIDED RIVERS DIALOGUE

Openness and Inconclusivity in Interpretation in Narrative Inquiry: Dimensions of the Social/Personal

Elaine:

In order to think further about perspective in narrative, I want to share a piece written by Stefinee Pinnegar following the editors' invitation to respond to the metaphor of the braided rivers that is included in the Introduction of this volume.

> When my brother was in dental school in San Francisco and we were both young and single, I went to visit him. On that visit we joined a group of other twentyish single people on a canoe trip down the Russian River. The river was swift in some places and calm in others and the river widened and narrowed as it wandered across the landscape. Periodically large metal objects with spiked ends that looked like the jacks used in the children's game of jacks crisscrossed the river to reduce erosion.
>
> There were about 30 of us divided into singles, pairs and trios paddling canoes. As we began the trip a challenge to confront and tip over other canoes was issued. During the next three hours, my brother, a competitive soul, diligently challenged and tipped over every canoe in the group. As we rounded the last bend of the trip, we were confronted by a human chain and our canoe was capsized. I found myself caught in the current rushing toward one of the large, spiky metal objects. No matter how hard I swam, I couldn't extract myself from the current. Every time I turned my head to gasp air, I shouted to my brother, "HELP! Nick, HELP." But no help came. Just moments from disaster, at the edge of my consciousness, I heard a voice and finally I paused to listen. I heard my brother yelling, "Stand Up! Stand Up! Stand Up!" When I stood up, the current of water that had held me fast, came only to my knees.
>
> As I thought of the braided river metaphor, I thought of how we get caught in our own interpretations of experience and channeled into well-worn paths of interpretation and action and we act in reflex seeing no other way to behave beyond the cultural patterns we have inherited, but in those moments when our understandings would lead us to act in ways we are not happy with we could stop and listen and stand up and see that as in the image of the metaphor there are patterns of action available and that if we consider our experience carefully we might also forge new pathways of interpretation and action.

Stefinee's retelling of a canoeing experience with her brother and friends when she felt panicked, terrified that she was in a situation beyond what she could handle, brought to mind the critical role of perspective in interpreting an incident or event in research and beyond. In her retelling, Stefinee described how, when at the point of despair, she heard her brother call out to her to stand up; upon doing just that, she realized that the water she had imagined in her mind to be very deep and treacherous to be just around knee-high and that the level of danger she had perceived was not matched by the actual circumstances of the situation.

As I read this response, I was reminded of the importance of alternative perspectives in narrative inquiry. As researchers, it is sometimes more comfortable to want to come to conclusions, to make assumptions about participants with whom we have been working for a long period of time, to have answers to our research questions, and to feel a degree of confidence in the interpretations that we attach to events observed in a research site or in response to something our participants have told us. Stefinee's response reminded me of the nature of interpretation – that it is, by nature, tentative, and highly influenced by circumstances of space, time, and interaction. The inconclusivity of the work is a quality to be valued, respected, and appreciated in that it keeps us open to possibilities of alternative perspectives.

This difference in perspective brings me back to the metaphor of the braided rivers presented in the Introduction. We have spoken about the interconnections between the chapters in this volume as being similar to the idea of the braided rivers, with some ideas and interpretations connecting like parts of the river where they join with other streams, and others ideas branching off in the way that some streams of the river break off to join other waterways. The idea of differences in perspective might be likened to the way in which the visual image of the braided rivers differs depending on the perspective from which one sees the river. From a bird's eye view, the coming together and branching off of the rivers is seen clearly as a body of connections, but from the ground where the birds roost for the evening, the definition of the streams of the river are not seen; rather, the focus shifts to the muddy banks and shallow waters where the birds roost. These differences in perspective are crucial from a researcher perspective.

This image came to mind as I thought about Mary Lynn's reflection upon her interactions with her students where she wonders if she has offended her students to the point that they would not be open to hearing her ideas about something that might be of relevance or even assistance to them. These thoughts arise in Candace and Elaine's chapter as they explore the role of culture in interpreting field notes, in Dixie and Cheryl's writing as they explore the role of betrayal in learning, and in Shaun, Vicki, and Janice's writing as they explore the role of past stories in contributing to their current understanding of their work with their students. As teachers and teacher educators, we bring to our work with our students our own perceptions of how we might engage our students in our subject area content. Differences, of course, arise in the process, as shaped by our prior experiences of teaching and being taught, but in the process of attempting to engage our students, we may inadvertently offend them. Mary Lynn's question about whether we might have offended our students to the extent that they may not be open to hearing what we have to offer raises questions of engagement and vulnerability in teaching and teacher education.

- What is the balance between sharing our experiences with our students and expecting them to dig into their own schooling histories to inform their teaching and work with their students when there is the possibility that in the process, they may become vulnerable to the criticism of their peers and/or teachers, or vulnerable to the feelings and sensitivities that may surface?
- What is the balance between establishing a classroom context that invites and encourages critical thought, and one that is safe?
- What is the balance between doing what students are comfortable with and what the instructors feel the students need?
- What does it mean to be ethical in teaching and teacher education?

Responses to these questions highlight the role of vulnerability in teaching and in being taught.

Dixie:
Elaine, I so appreciate how you have elaborated on perspective and the ethics of teaching and teacher education. As you brought forward the additional images of the "bird's eye view" versus the view from the birds' roosting place, I thought of my time mired in the mud when I wrote of my place in our chapter. Cheryl, in her response, effectively shared with me the "bird's eye view" which I needed both professionally and emotionally. Stefinee's analogy of standing up in the river is another stirring image that we sometimes need a more knowledgeable other to enhance our awareness and to help us develop a new, different perspective.

Vicki:
I, too, see this idea of perspective – as captured in the image of the cranes' seeing from above or in the muck – as conceptually linked to the burrowing

and broadening framework that Dixie and Cheryl use to construct their understandings of place.

I, too, was profoundly touched by wonderings of Mary Lynn and Stefinee regarding the way that teacher candidates are characterized in education literature. My sense is that, Elaine, when you speak of "subject matter" with which you engage your students, similar to Mary Lynn, what you are referring to is culture. I hear your deep resonance with Mary Lynn's concern. This concern about the betrayal that you wonder might be read into the characterizations of teachers (and teacher candidates) that litter the education literature is worrisome and widespread. You tug at it from your position working in multicultural education. I am uncomfortable with this same pattern of making sweeping generalization about teachers and teachers' knowledge in the mathematics education literature. It hints at the idea brought up in conversations related to the notion of place about betrayal. In one sense, we – as members of that discourse community are betraying our students – and, at the same time, we are in relationship with them hoping to enliven with them our "best loved selves" (Dewey's idea, not my own).

And, then, I wonder about ourselves and the sense of betrayal I sometimes sense when I listen to policy makers disparage the work we are all engaged in as teacher educators. Maybe this sense of betrayal helps us to know "the place" of the College of Education.

CHAPTER TWO

BURROWING AND BROADENING IN THE STORIED PLACE OF TEACHER EDUCATION

Dixie Keyes and Cheryl Craig

ABSTRACT

Purpose – *The purpose of this chapter is to demonstrate "walking alongside" in the three-dimensional space of narrative inquiry, as explored through the field texts of two teacher educators, one mentoring the other through layered stories of "place."*

Approach – *The authors use several interpretive tools to explore the question, "What sustains us as teacher educators?" The dialogue deepens as the authors make their professional knowledge landscapes more visible, bringing sacred stories, stories of gender, stories of hierarchy, stories of power, and stories of race forward, exploring how these stories are held in tension with one another. The authors ponder the questions: what happens when the small stories' educators living in "place" become so far removed from authorized meta-narratives also underway in "place"? And, how can we remain wakeful to the numerous story constellations of others that revolve around us?*

Findings – *The analytical spaces described by the researchers helped them to realize and share with others that researchers may more fully respect the vulnerability our research participants feel that comes along with their own restorying*. Vulnerability brought forward a common bond found in the experiences of "place" in the field texts. Narrative inquirers who write field texts, then restory their own narratives of place, add to the empirical dimensions of narrative inquiry and its attentiveness to lived experience.

Research implications – *This demonstration, through its examples of the three-dimensional space of narrative inquiry, shows how interpretation emanates from the various cracks, corners, and even the air within this important analytical space. Narrative researchers may continue to unpack this space in their work. Narrative inquirers are also reminded that place is storied and that human beings are narratively anchored in place, an important consideration for relational research ethics.*

Value – *Readers can interact with the tools used by narrative inquirers, in this case, "tracing" and "burrowing and broadening." Narrative inquirers may also recognize vulnerability as an effect of interpreting within the three-dimensional inquiry space, and understand the necessity of vulnerability as a part of thinking narratively.*

Keywords: Narrative inquiry; vulnerability; teacher education identity; relational research ethics; three-dimensional narrative inquiry space

INTRODUCTION

Researchers Walking Alongside

We, Dixie and Cheryl, situated ourselves alongside one another over 2 years ago, specifically to restory our stories of place and collect them, thereby creating field texts about our lives as teacher educators. Our history together began in 2002 when we first met, Cheryl as one of Dixie's professors from the University of Houston's doctoral program, and Dixie, a full-time high school English teacher who still had 4 more years of coursework, research, and writing to do before she graduated. By situating ourselves together again, we actually demonstrate the aspects of the three-dimensional inquiry space: we explored our places in detail (which was our specific task and purpose), and we also found ourselves living temporally (backwards and forwards, inside and outside) with our histories as teachers and teacher educators. Sociality also wove into the narratives shared in this chapter as we explored our vulnerabilities of place and self. Through writing our field texts, which renewed our time of walking alongside once again, Dixie found herself "tracing" for the purpose of meaning-making. This narrative tool, demonstrated in this work, not only allowed her to live alongside Cheryl, but reminded her of experiences of living alongside other research participants who did the same thing, maybe in different ways. Narrative inquirers who write field texts then restory their own narratives of place, can lay these alongside the participants as research texts, which adds to the empirical dimensions of narrative inquiry and its attentiveness to lived experience. We hope our demonstration of this provides examples of the three-dimensional space of narrative inquiry and how interpretation emanates from the various cracks, corners, and even the air within this important analytical space.

Demonstrated in the field texts that follow are empathy and understanding created by Dixie's first small stories of place, then Cheryl's that are far removed from the grand narratives underway in our places. Vulnerability brought forward a common bond found in the experiences of "place" in these field texts. The analytical space Dixie and Cheryl found helped them to realize and share with others that researchers may more fully respect the vulnerability our research participants feel that comes along with their own restorying we ask them to bring forward in the research relationship.

A Mentor in Burrowing and Broadening

Dixie found herself bringing forward or unpacking stories of the sociopolitical dimensions of her place, both as an institution and in relationship to others in the same place (colleagues, administrators, students). Key to this was that these were *her* institutional stories as opposed to stories *of* her institution. They were *her* "teacher educator self" stories rather than stories *of* her "teacher educator self" (Clandinin & Connelly, 1996). She found herself feeling a strong voice and wanting to pronounce her perspectives through the tracings presented; maybe other beginning teacher educators want and need such advocacy. She needed to share these stories and collect them through the tool of tracing in order to interpret her place and to move forward to new understandings of place. She needed to respect and excavate the "tensions" found, one with the other through burrowing and broadening. Cheryl, her mentor, helped move her forward to do this, provoking wakefulness, which led to additional spaces for interpretation.

This process is made visible in the two-part "Burrowing and Broadening" that follows. First is Dixie's collection of stories of place, written from 2007 to 2010, centered in the sociopolitical dimensions of her place in higher education as a beginning teacher educator. This writing became a field text with its origins in her personal journaling when she was invited to write about her place as a teacher educator by the group of narrative inquirers involved in this volume. She used tracing to bring her teacher educator self stories to one place for interpretation, unpacking her sense of place, and offering the vulnerable roots of a tense existence in this place to Cheryl, an experienced researcher and leader in the field of teacher education, for response. This process is exemplified through Bateson's reflections on a Mobius strip:

> To get outside of the imprisoning framework of assumptions learned within a single tradition, habits of attention and interpretation need to be stretched and pulled and folded back upon themselves, life lived upon a Mobius strip. These lessons are far too complex for a single encounter, achieved by garnering doubled and often contradictory visions rather than by replacing one set of ideas with another. (Bateson, 1994, p. 43)

By folding back upon our pasts, we possessed our narratives of place and hoped for newfound understandings. Bateson understood this connection. "... the retelling [of a private memory] exemplifies the making of a connection from one pattern to another" (p. 11). We harvest learning in "what I already know ... getting more and more juice" from past events (Bateson, 2000, p. 229) (Fig. 1).

PART 1: "WHAT SUSTAINS YOU?" THE TRACINGS OF A TEACHER EDUCATOR – DIXIE KEYES

Entering the "Field of Possibles" – Finding the Rifts and Gaps

In one of her essays (1995), Maxine Greene discussed education and literacy in terms of those in power who have access as opposed to those who are

Fig. 1. A Mobius Strip.

Burrowing and Broadening in the Storied Place of Teacher Education 27

Fig. 2. Dixie's Illustrated Tracings on One Page.

marginalized in various ways who do not or cannot share in defined literacies of power. She wrote, "Yes becoming literate is also a matter of transcending the given, of entering a field of possibles. We are moved to do that, however, only when we become aware of rifts, gaps in what we think of as reality." As she described how she directly challenged herself to think about her own thinking, she concluded, "This meant singling out determining factors in my life—the seductions as well as the controls" (pp. 111–112).

In my attempts of "transcending the given and entering a field of possibles," I unpack the "rifts" in my life as a teacher educator and narrative researcher. As I and other narrative inquirers move toward making visible the analytic and interpretive processes involved in developing narrative understandings of teacher educator identity, I began restorying narratives from the past 2 years. In a book chapter (Keyes, 2011), I wrote of a tool I discovered as a narrative inquirer – a conceptualization I named "tracing." The tool of tracing allows me to more specifically describe my process of reproducing various storied images together from separate contexts and histories, effectively bringing them together to one central location – just as a child might trace three or four images of interest onto one piece of paper. Although I used tracing to make sense of the temporal nature of stories in my field texts, it appeared valuable to me in making sense of my own experiences as I collected or sketched them in one place for the purpose of sense-making (see the depiction of tracing above). The traced stories, memories, moments, thoughts, and events collected in this writing guided me in addressing an important question posed at a narrative symposium by Jean Clandinin (Keyes, journal notes, 2010), "What sustains you as a teacher educator?" (Fig. 2)

Tracing One: A Narrative of Place

One of the veteran professors in my department invited a number of colleagues to a local restaurant downtown ... the kind that has an "upstairs" where one can get a dirty martini and a good beer in a dry county in the Southern United States. Sitting in a corner, listening to a potential American Idol playing guitar and singing, I heard my colleague/friend once again make references to the "Golden Age" of the Department of Teacher Education at our university. "We used to have 19 graduate assistants, one assigned to each of us!" she commented. Another veteran faculty member of 22 years stated, "and all of the summer teaching we wanted. We had 30 people in each section of our junior courses, and 15 in the field classes."

I found it easy to separate myself and my viewpoints from these senior faculty members as a 4-year neophyte in the department. Yet, they had taken me under their wings in subtle ways over those 4 years, recommending various committees and assigning me tasks to help me understand governance and curriculum, but I had not yet understood, until tonight, that they missed the "golden days" where teacher educators were respected as were theories of learning and teaching. They understood the organic nature of learning and how good teachers respond to the evolution of relationships among the students and between the students and themselves. I realized they had been preparing me all along for the many adventures of politics, curriculum feuds, and bargaining that has to happen if one wants to stay in this profession.

Veteran or beginner, we are all currently taking swings from the politicians who want alternative licensure to prepare most teachers, who value content knowledge and ignore the complexities of personal practical knowledge and experience (Clandinin & Connelly, 2000). And I left the evening feeling even more a part of the teacher education family.

Tracing Two: What Sustains You?

Jean Clandinin posed a question during a narrative symposium at the 2010 American Educational Research Association (AERA) conference, which had actually become a personal inquiry for me since early May. "What sustains you?" she asked after she read our papers dealing with teacher and teacher educator tensions and understandings. "What keeps you going in these turbulent times?" That question seemed formed just for me and like a detective with a good lead, it found a gap, a space to investigate. I had no answer that day, the next week, or the next.

So, I had to think about it awhile, especially after attending several presidential sessions at AERA where the smartest educators and researchers in our country were sharing with us that politics dominate the decisions of accountability and curriculum these days ... although these prolific minds were producing and publishing the writing and research that promote foundations of learning and teaching and facets of literacy that facilitate lifelong learning; the politicians and think-tanks in power simply choose the other – they choose research that spotlights alternative licensure for teachers (with its own political circle) – and throw it toward the media, and suddenly society leans toward thinking that teacher education programs are bad, in need of repair or dissolution, and that anyone can become a teacher if they have content expertise.

Tracing Three: I Want to be a Teacher – The Politics of Getting There

I was listening to National Public Radio one morning, to a former stockbroker who lost his job on Wall Street and decided to become a math teacher in New Jersey. He found an alternative licensure program called "From Traders to Teachers," went to an informative meeting, and signed on. Once he committed to the program, he had to take the state content exam for licensure purposes, and also had to return to his university to take additional math courses. He lamented during his interview his surprise at how hard the math exam was, that it contained trigonometry, and that he thought he had failed. After finding out he passed, he continued his lament about having to take additional math courses and how he had to spend several weekends away from his family to study for them during the summer. I listened in disbelief realizing that most of society has no idea of the rigor of conventional teacher education programs ... they don't realize there is an entire body of literature on how people learn things, and that it threads out into important concepts like multicultural education, literacy-based learning, second-language learner methodologies, multiple intelligences and learning styles, democratic classroom management, processes of writing, reading and writing across content areas ... all of the concepts involved in our teacher education program. Add to that the ways in which teachers and teacher educators are curriculum makers, on complex landscapes where the lives of students are the curriculum ... will this former stockbroker understand?

I now know what people mean when they speak of "putting the politics aside." I always thought of the various agendas of politicians, that they were generally working for the good of the people. After 4 years in higher education, I understand now that "politics" often means either finding ways to keep one's job or finding ways to make more money. Politics means taking care of oneself and one's friends, whereby the goal or mission of the department or college can be lost. My problem is I entered the career of a teacher educator taking a pay cut from my public school position and that I really wanted to be of service, to write, and to work with teacher candidates and share my experiences with them. Instead, I spend probably 30% of my time dealing with politics and bargaining at committee tables where everyone around it has a particular personal agenda and everyone knows it.

Tracing Four: Batting in a Darkened Field

In my second year as a teacher education faculty member, I found myself positioned on a governance council – not an involvement I had asked for, but a supplemental position involved in a committee representation. I had just written two courses for our masters reading program, which I had successfully passed through this governance system. Upon my attendance at the second meeting of this council, we were presented with a graduate course proposal that seemed scant to me. Not fully comprehending the in-depth political situation of membership on this council, I asked a question about the proposal, which listed only five topics for this graduate course vs. the usually required 14 weeks of topics. Only five topics were listed because another department's programs were switching to a privatized, online course format where each course could only be five weeks long; hence, only five topics were needed. After I asked why only five topics were presented, the key administrator became agitated, responding in a raised voice and with a raised finger. I was appalled; I thought my previous experiences in writing graduate courses along with the logical way I asked the question was quite relevant to the task of the committee. Although, as a teacher, I had worked for principals who would let me know why something just could not happen, after 12 years of attaining my education and three degrees specializing in this field, I never thought I would be dealing with these obvious political issues that precluded any sincere questions posed, which would benefit the program.

I had entered the playing field of some game I did not fully understand. No one was presenting me with the rules of play, and I found myself holding a bat in a dark field where I could see no one. The scoreboard was obscured, but I began to pull together the distant voices of the veteran professors, some of my mentors, my gut feelings about what was right, and what my intentions were for myself in the position of a teacher educator.

Tracing Five: Taking Action – How?

I'll add another event to my sketchpad. A month ago, I found myself advising two individuals – one a public school teacher not getting along with her principal and the other a new full-time, Pete Seeger-loving instructor at our university trying to enact service learning components in the English as second-language program without informing his department chair. I found myself giving advice of "Give yourself time to get over the emotions of the relationship, and consider opening space for dialogue with your administrator. Smile even though you don't feel like it. Be positive although you've been agitated or dismissed, and go have a focused, professional talk about your hopes, desires, and plans for your students. Then ask them for their help and advocacy."

I suppose I've realized that each of us carries our own hopes, desires, and plans within, and we do not take the time to consider that somebody else's may differ from our own. This may seem obvious, but we do not often consider it when we make decisions, take action, or begin a project. So if one administrator's hopes or plans center on enhancing the professional growth of teachers at that school, and you have taken charge of your own professional growth without advice or input from that administrator, then that could build tension. But by opening dialogue and being transparent about your plans, you could find an advocate to help you along your journey. Is this playing the game, or is it building valuable professional relationships?

I shared with one of these people that some days I can do this and some days I simply cannot. One thing I do know, though, is that the National Writing Project grant I direct is important to lots of teachers and their students, so if my department chair asks me to go to lunch or wants me to chair a particular committee, more than likely I will go to lunch although I planned to work through it, or I will chair the committee because I know I want to ask for a few hundred dollars of matching funds related to the grant.

So, What Sustains Me?

So, what sustains me? A note from a 40ish female preservice teacher in my literature class, who seems to be beginning her second life with a second husband and a second career, who shared with me, "I've never learned this way before." An e-mail from a preservice teacher who successfully passed her state licensure exam (the one on pedagogy) and took the time to send me a message saying she passed because of my course – the one that focuses on learning theory and effective teaching. Another that comes to mind is from a former teacher candidate with a teaching position in another state who was attempting to enter into a masters program in teaching and learning. "I got in … " she e-mailed, thanking me for the recommendation. Then there was the listserve proclamation from one of our state literacy organization board members about the state anthology I co-edit. He mentioned the "inestimable impact" of this publication and detailed the reaction of one of his published students: "The look of sheer satisfaction on the face of a student who's reading his very first published work is proof enough for me!" Another teacher declared that a poem published in the state anthology was the only thing her student took seriously all year long. My cup began to slosh.

Or maybe it was the phone call from a first-year teacher who was a former student and who had attended our writing institute before she began her first job. She let me know that 30 of her 60 students had moved from "Below Basic" in math to either "Proficient" or "Advanced" on the state math benchmark test. How did this happen? Because she studied, understood, and valued the need for interactive learning, for manipulatives and connections to real life, and for differentiated instruction – all learned in our traditional teacher education program. Although I have just begun to collect answers to Jean Clandinin's question, it seems as if this collection lies in the lived experiences that surround me as a teacher educator.

Just like there is an underground, invisible, organic connection among trees, in nature – ecosystems we do not often pay attention to unless there is an oil spill or a volcanic eruption ... there is an underground, invisible, often undecipherable system in each individual in a classroom and in the environment created by a teacher and the group of students with whom she works and lives. We, as humans, tend to forget about these living systems because we are so busy attending to our own agendas. Somebody wants a job with good health insurance; somebody lost their first-choice career; somebody wants to get tenure; somebody wants legislation to pass so they can promote a program in which they have investments. That kind of business eats away at my soul and depletes the goodness in my cup.

Tracing Six: Forced Reinterpretation of Place

In 2009, the US Secretary of Education, Arnie Duncan, began holistically blasting teacher education programs without full knowledge of their rigor, processes, or identities (Field, 2009). I began to consistently read of his political agenda that will reward some teachers and school districts and leave others behind. After the backlash he received from multiple sources, he recognized that successful teacher education programs do exist, but he still persists in pushing funding of alternative licensure programs as businesses that will "prepare" teachers from other careers who have been found to leave the teaching profession soon after they begin. This conduit forces teacher educators to reinterpret their place and to think more deeply about the lenses of curriculum in teacher education programs. In order to advocate for teacher education programs and for teachers, it is time to decide what sustains me, and it is time to decide to write and share about it more often.

So, I accepted an invitation to speak to an already-gathered group of local school administrators, blending a talk on 21st century skills with my version of "invest in your teachers and know they are curriculum makers." I found myself pointing to specific lines from the Common Core Standards introduction, which acknowledges that the new national standards do not define how teachers should teach, nor do they describe all that can or should be taught. And I included an iteration of Cheryl Craig citing Joseph

Schwab: Teachers are "fountainheads of the curricular decision" (Schwab, 1983, p. 241). They "*must* be involved in debate, deliberation, and decision about what and how to teach" (Schwab, 1983, p. 245, italics in original).

Knowing the administrators in the room to have varied agendas and contexts, I could feel my points hitting home with some, while others had wrinkled foreheads, seeming more critical about believing in their teachers instead of requiring canned curriculum from them. One seemed very concerned about students learning to read and write cursive, as opposed to the issue of moving forward with 21st-century technology skills. I always tell myself in such moments of tensions and ambiguity that maybe I am prying open a little space for thought or ideas, or planting a seed that somebody else might water, and that listeners might think more critically about matters of curriculum instead of taking the usual or reductionistic view. Instead of interpreting important movements like the national standards movement into another formula for testing, I hoped they would see this new curriculum framework as a skeleton of the "what," while teachers and students are the "how" and the "why." Through participation in this event with school administrators, I realized not only how multiple interpretations were present within this national standards movement but also how those interpretations did not yet involve teachers.

Tracing Seven: Vulnerability

Last on the sketchpad for now, an event more recent, from my fifth year as a teacher educator, what I call a "free verse moment," I often write free verse poetry about fascinating moments or observations that happen in ordinary places – the gym, a museum, an airport, a sidewalk. This moment happened on an elevator at the Peabody Hotel in Little Rock. I was riding the elevator down to the lobby with four teacher friends of mine. After a long day at a state conference, we were heading to a sushi restaurant across the street. Two distinguished-looking gentlemen in suits and ties had previously entered the elevator, and they welcomed us aboard. Seeing my conference nametag that also listed my university's name, one of the men said he had met another professor from my university today. Then he said, "I'm in curriculum." I smiled and responded, "So am I – at least I try," in a polite, self-deprecating way.

"I'm the Dean of the ... department at ... and the director of the STEM center there," he added, surprising me with this specific hierarchy of information. He continued to speak of his work in educating practicing teachers of the national standards. The elevator door opened, and the seven of us stepped out. I ended up walking beside this Dean and could not refrain from saying, "Teachers have all the answers ... we should listen to them more often," my teacher friends in earshot. The two men were non-responsive. Five seconds passed, and as we all walked through the automatic glass doors that opened magically for the polished Dean (or maybe it was for the teachers!), his voice boomeranged, "As long as what they think matches the standards." Then *I* was non-responsive, and our two groups moved in different directions down the street.

"Y'know, he's wrong," I addressed to my friends a few steps forward. "You all do have the answers, and you need to voice to people like him that you do." As I responded to my teacher friends, I could not help but pay attention to the feeling of intimidation that had passed through me during this interaction with the distinguished Dean. He reminded me of my past encounter in the governance council with the politically motivated administrator, a symbol of polished power, someone who probably lives far from students and teachers in classrooms. I felt vulnerable in opposition to his firm thoughts, knowing that my teacher friends heard such thoughts on a daily basis from the conduits on their professional landscapes, and that they often absorbed such thoughts about curriculum. My position seemed a distant voice or echo people think they may have heard, but not quite.

I thought back to a *Teaching and Teacher Education* journal article I read last year, about teacher emotions and educational reform (Kelchtermans, 2005). Kelchtermans posited a conceptual stance toward the emotions of teachers and the role these emotions play in educational change and reform. Specifically, he described the "intense emotions" teachers have toward reform policies because they immediately and directly impact the relationships they have with their students, "the very heart of teaching" (p. 999). My notes in the margins of the article read, "I can teach preservice teachers about vulnerability and sense of identity before they have their own classrooms," thinking of how I could incorporate Kelchtermans' important premise.

Kelchtermans saw vulnerability as a structural condition in education. An hour after the elevator ride – the free verse moment – I wrote in my journal

Along the Continuum

Slick, gray hair and sharp, crisp brows – expensive suit and tie, unwrinkled by the conference day.
Frizzy hair unkempt, tired feet in $9 shoes, I like he, a connoisseur of curriculum.
"Teachers have the answers," the words left my mouth.

> "As long as they meet the standards," the words left his.
> He a director, I a lover of the swamp.
> He, in the airplane above, and I trudging below.
> "It's amazing how those in the field of education live in different plotlines on the continuum," I shared with a friend.
> Never had I been so aware of myself in the murky depths below,
> living in vulnerability yet gleaning such
> marvelous meaning
> from the juxtaposition
> in the elevator.

I realized that meaning comes to me from my trek in the mud, from living in the lowlands, and from being vulnerable to determine my voice. Is it possible that this is what sustains me? Can vulnerability be my sustenance? Can I learn to revel in certain vulnerability, knowing that the preservice teachers with whom I work bring their stories back to me?

> ... it is this inescapable vulnerability that ultimately constitutes the very possibility for teachers to "educate" and to teach in a way that really makes a difference in students' lives. Policy makers—as well as the technocratic educationalists who eagerly assist them—would benefit from acknowledging these fundamental complexities in teacher and being a teacher ... In the end it is the teachers, the women and men in the classroom, who determine whether good schooling actually "happens." (Kelchtermans, 2005, p. 1005)

As Cheryl's response challenges me, maybe us all, to be awake to the positioning of small stories of place that seem so distant from the "authorized meta-narratives" also underway, I am provoked to empathy, to not only be awake, but to rise to meet the narratives of others and to take a hopeful watch for the stories of others that fold back into my own.

Let me end by returning to Maxine Greene's (1995) essay. "We have to be articulate enough and able to exert ourselves to name what we see around us—the hunger, the passivity, the homelessness, the 'silences'" (p. 112).

PART 2: A RESPONSE TO "WHAT SUSTAINS YOU?" – CHERYL CRAIG

Dixie Keyes, my former doctoral student, has addressed in Part 1 the research puzzle, "What sustains you?" and burrowed into it – in the narrative inquiry vernacular (Connelly & Clandinin, 1990). The research puzzle originated with a question posed by my former doctoral advisor, Jean Clandinin, in 2010 at the American Educational Research Meeting. I immediately found myself engaged in broadening, another of narrative inquiry's interpretive tools, as I found myself transported over time to two different places: the University of Alberta in Canada, specifically the Centre for Research for Teacher Education and Development, my academic homeplace, the place from which I graduated, and the University of Texas at Brownsville where I taught Dixie in an off-campus cohort to help establish that campus's academic presence in the city bordering Mexico. Yet, neither of these places is the place where I now work, which is the University of Houston, the place that for more than a decade has shaped my knowing of academia.

So, Dixie's tracings – prompted by Jean's query – caused me to reflectively travel from place to place, all of which are distinctively different: The University of Alberta, one of Canada's leading research institutions, situated in the largest most northern city in Canada; The University of Texas at Brownsville, which is located in the most economically underserved region of the United States, and the University of Houston, also a huge high research intensive university, one located in the heart of the fourth largest city of America, a metropolis with some of the most extreme contrasts between wealth and poverty anywhere in the world. Hence, it is with this dizzying sense of knowing these particular places (coupled with my own rural background), and coming to a fourth place, post-Hurricane New Orleans where the AERA meeting was held in 2011, that I come to this interpretive act. I know fully well that I am grappling to find a "commonplace of experience" (Lane, 1988) with Dixie – whose work life now unfolds in a regional university in Arkansas – and with readers, whose places I simply do not know. Of course, the commonplace we all share, whether our universities are located in the north – like the University of Alberta, or in the south – like the University of Houston or the University of Texas at Brownsville, is academia. And I believe the research puzzle Jean Clandinin was drawing to the forefront – and the one to which Dixie was responding is: "How do we keep going amid the craziness going on around us in the places where our academic work unfurls?" This question is a particularly fitting one to address as Dixie has done in Part 1.

As foreshadowed, Dixie launched her paper with broadening – she did so by offering a story of the "golden years" of teacher education known by others at her place of work. I personally have not experienced that era, but many of the professors with whom I work (and who Dixie knows) have, and they, too, speak of the "glory days" of my College of Education. I resonate with Dixie's story as I lay my story alongside hers: I, too, found myself working at a place laden with stories – a place rich in social–historical detail. Many may know that, at one point, the University of Houston was the main campus for teacher education in the region and a leading source of US educational policy making where teacher education was concerned. Now, there are 34 competitors established in the city limits; the University of Houston is the 14th producer of total teacher education graduates according to the Texas Coordinating Board's list. And I, like Dixie, have had polite conversations with others about what is going on. Not long ago, a powerful city representative asked me: "Do you ever get the feeling that teacher education is being shut down?" "The idea has crossed my mind," I responded. "When I first came to the campus 10 years ago, there were at least 60 ranked professors in my department ... and that was about two decades *after* the department's rise to fame." Then, my voice trailed: "I think we may have about 15 tenured faculty left."

Arriving in Houston, it did not take me long to realize that knowing about the history of segregation/desegregation in the American South and living/studying alongside people who have experienced and breathed it their entire lives are enormously different matters. For example, the first campus where I conducted research was located in one of the wealthiest White neighborhoods in the United States (i.e., Craig, 2001), whereas my second research site was located in the second largest underserved Black communities in the United States (i.e., Craig, 2006a). I will always recall my South Korean doctoral student who visited two schools with me for the first time and quietly asked: "Why do Black kids have to line up for lunch and walk without speaking under close supervision? ... And why do White kids not have to do so?"

And, in the years following the campuses I have described, came another research site, a school filled with largely Mexican/South American immigrant children who were thriving because the place featured a dual language program that allowed them to simultaneously learn Spanish, their language of birth, and English, their adopted language. And, I was at that place when the attitude toward immigrants and additive approaches to language instruction fell into disfavor in Arizona and the news spread like wild fire to Texas. Hearing the rancorous debate on radio and television talk shows, the immigrant parents, even in the face of their children's positive growth, begged for English-only instruction in Texas as a way to avoid broken relationships and risk possible job loss (Craig, 2009). So it isn't just that places are historically, geographically, socially, and politically situated, but that stories travel from place to place – Margaret Olson and I called these traveling stories (Olson & Craig, 2009a) in a 2009 *Teachers College Record* article – with the stories of one place having a shaping effect on the stories of another place through the narratives people carry back and forth.

But I have wandered as I have opened up the aperture of my lens, this time mingling my research experiences with my teaching experiences to make the professional knowledge landscape (Clandinin & Connelly, 1995) in which I work more visible ... But I want to return to Dixie's interactions with her department colleagues. I want to lay a personal story beside her narrative. I have often shared with Dixie that one of the things I worry about is whether I have prepared my graduate students for life in the context of academia, which is a much different task than preparing them to be researchers and teachers. Where Dixie is concerned, I would refine the question ever further – life in academia as a female living in the American south – particularly since Dixie was in an off-campus cohort being taught by many of the people whose stories brushed against mine. For example, was she awoken to the sacred stories (Clandinin & Connelly, 1995) within which her education was taking place? Did she notice the story of gender and how I was the only female professor who taught her? Was she aware of the story of race and how all of us, being White, represented the campus with the most diverse student population in the United States? Did she notice the story of hierarchy and how the males were full professors and I was not? Could she see the story of power and how some student–professor relationships were based on the likelihood of future grant and contract opportunities? Was she acquainted with the story of merit and how merit increases can be achieved – not through teaching, research and scholarship, but through the story of affiliation? Did she know that grants and contracts could be accessed the same way? Concurrently, did she note also that none of these stories of place were fixed – that they were in constant motion, with priorities frequently fluctuating, dependent on the situation that arose and the people involved? Was she aware of the constant storying and restorying (Connelly & Clandinin, 1990) going on? For example, I am now almost assured merit increases because many in my department consider curriculum and instruction to be in competition with the educational psychology department. Engaging in that larger competition is currently more important than keeping me in my place in the department, which seemed to be more of a priority when Dixie was a student and I was not a full professor. Also, in this case, I, like Dixie, did not fictionalize my account, which is another of narrative inquiry's interpretive devices, but chose instead to raise questions that made issues visible while keeping an ethical stance at the forefront of the inquiry.

As I burrowed into the blurred details of my place and Dixie's possible reading of it, I suspected the answer was no. And Dixie confirmed that I was correct. My sense was Dixie was like me and others I know: unable to fully grasp issues until such issues have been experienced first-hand or vicariously through a close other. Schwab, who reportedly had a troubled childhood, said in one of the documents contained in the University of Chicago archives (see Schwab, 2007) that people do not grow up until they have been betrayed. I have often wondered whether we do not come to know place until several such betrayals have taken place. I put that idea out there as something for us to think about as I now, as a narrative inquirer, broaden in a different way, through weaving in the literature and connecting the curricular with the psychological and the social.

And, while I am unpacking stories of place, I want to tuck in one difference in place to which I have awakened that may or may not be a Canadian-American or perhaps a Southern US thing. In the hallways, my colleagues and I discuss problems in the college/problems in the public schools, etc. However, whenever we have formal meetings and I, coming from a different place, try to raise issues – even issues with which others fully agree in informal spaces – we are never able to discuss them. Instead, we seem to revert to the "how great we are" cover story (Clandinin & Connelly, 1995; Olson & Craig, 2005) – which allows the thin veneer of "everything is okay" to continue while systematically avoiding any matter that might disrupt the plotline of past grandeur, despite the fact that only a mere thread of it remains.

I suspect Dixie was already living the secret story (Clandinin & Connelly, 1995) of deriving satisfaction/feeling sustained in place through living and learning productively alongside her students when she became a doctoral student. However, what I suspect her work with me did was provide her with the language for an image of teaching – that of teacher as curriculum maker (Clandinin & Connelly, 1992; Craig & Ross, 2008) – which she already lived and gave her terms such as Donald's Schön's (1983) high ground of theory and "swampy lowlands" of practice, which, I concur with Dixie, are vicarious places that powerfully shape how and what we know. And, Dixie, already being an English teacher and viewing the world narratively, easily found value in the narrative inquiry method because it resonated with her knowing of past places over time.

So, "What sustains me?" "What keeps me going in these turbulent times?" Let me now personally burrow into this puzzle. Like Dixie, it is my students and the people with whom I am acquainted. It is the small stories given back to me – everything from "something you said influenced my thinking" to "you changed my life – I will never be the same." It is the teacher whose daughter was tragically killed in a car accident who courageously studied "teaching and grief"; it is the statistician turned narrative inquirer with whom I wrangled often; it's the physician whose awarded dissertation on doctor–patient relationships made front-page news; it is my research participants and their students who say they miss me when I am not with them. And more recently, I can broaden my experiences to my international colleagues – the teacher who shed a tear during one of my talks in Hong Kong, the hard questions I was asked in Australia, and the human kindness I was shown in South Korea. All of this confirms for me that my humble attempts to touch eternity (to borrow Tom Barone's (2001) elegant term) have been acknowledged and that I, in all of my vulnerability, with all of my exposed flaws – am, in some, near-imperceptible way, making a difference in the lives of those with whom I am in relationship – in whatever work-related place that ends up being.

But I cannot end this interpretative discussion of place without underscoring a major concern about what happens when the small stories we are living in place become so far removed from authorized meta-narratives also underway in place. In another *Teachers College Record* article, Margaret Olson and I (Olson & Craig, 2009b) addressed that question. I will not speak for Margaret and her preservice teacher participant's experiences, but my in-service teacher participant, like Margaret's, left the profession and the underserved campus where he successfully taught mathematics to at-risk, minority youth. He simply was unable to bridge the divide between the differences he felt he was making in children's lives – and the stories that were given back to him by a chorus of others (parents, fellow teachers, students) – and the lack of effect attributed to him through the negative policy rhetoric of the US No Child Left Behind Act. A similar situation happened this year with the female beginning as a literacy teacher with whom I have worked in a different school district for six years. Her narrative also no longer sustained her as a teaching story to live by and similarly became a "story to leave by," to coin Clandinin, Downey, and Huber (2009) term.

To conclude, human beings are narratively anchored in place and part of many story constellations (Craig, 2007), some that we know relatively well (both reflectively and nonreflectively), and some that are only faintly visible to us. These sets of paired stories – whether they be stories of teachers/ teacher stories, stories of school/school stories (Clandinin & Connelly, 1996), stories of community/community stories (Craig, 2001), stories of policy/policy stories, stories of teacher self/teacher self stories (Craig, 2006b) – are all held in tension with one another. Such narratives can be interpreted through broadening, burrowing, and storying and restorying, as I have attempted to show in Part 2 in my response to Dixie's tracing that was presented in Part 1. Also, fictionalization can be used to blur circumstances and protect identities, although both Dixie and I chose to raise general questions in this instance in order to attend mindfully to ethical considerations. All of this suggests that place is storied, when we choose to be awaken to it, and hence, available to be interpreted, as Dixie and I – each in our own way – have attempted to show.

REFERENCES

Barone, T. (2001). *Touching eternity: The enduring outcomes of teaching.* New York, NY: Teachers College Press.
Bateson, M. C. (1994). *Peripheral visions: Learning along the way.* New York, NY: Harper Collins Publishers.
Bateson, M. C. (2000). *Full circles, overlapping lives: Culture and generation in transition.* New York, NY: Ballantine Books.
Clandinin, D. J., & Connelly, F. M. (1992). Teacher as curriculum maker. In P. Jackson (Ed.), *Handbook of curriculum* (pp. 363–461). New York, NY: Macmillan.
Clandinin, D. J., & Connelly, F. M. (1995). *Teachers' professional knowledge landscapes.* New York, NY: Teachers College Press.
Clandinin, D. J., & Connelly, F. M. (1996). Teachers' professional knowledge landscapes: Teacher stories-stories of teachers-school stories-stories of school. *Educational Researcher, 25*(5), 2–14.
Clandinin, D. J., & Connelly, F. M. (2000). *Narrative inquiry: Experience and story in qualitative research.* San Francisco, CA: Jossey-Bass.
Clandinin, D. J., Downey, C. A., & Huber, J. (2009). Attending to changing landscapes: Shaping the interwoven identities of teachers and teacher educators. *Asia-Pacific Journal of Teacher Education, 37*(2), 141–151.
Connelly, F. M., & Clandinin, D. J. (1990). Stories of experience and narrative inquiry. *Educational Researcher, 19*(5), 2–14.
Craig, C. (2001). The relationships between and among teacher knowledge, communities of knowing, and top down school reform: A case of "The Monkey's Paw". *Curriculum Inquiry, 31*(3), 303–331.
Craig, C. (2006a). Why is dissemination of knowledge so difficult? The nature of teacher knowledge and the spread of curriculum reform. *American Educational Research Journal, 43*(2), 257–293.
Craig, C. (2006b). Change, changing, and being changed: A self-study of a teacher educator's becoming real in the throes of urban school reform. *Studying Teacher Education, 2*(1), 105–116.
Craig, C. (2007). Story constellations: A narrative approach to situating teachers' knowledge of school reform in context. *Teaching and Teacher Education, 23*(2), 173–188.
Craig, C. (2009). The contested classroom space: A decade of lived education policy in Texas schools. *American Educational Research Journal, 46*(4), 1034–1059.
Craig, C., & Ross, V. (2008). Cultivating teachers as curriculum makers. In F. M. Connelly (Ed.), *Sage handbook of curriculum and instruction* (pp. 282–305). Thousand Oaks, CA: Sage.

Field, K. (2009). Education secretary praises teaching but criticizes teaching programs. *Chronicle of Higher Education*. Retrieved from http://chronicle.com/article/Education-Secretary-Praises/48779/. Accessed on October 2009.

Greene, M. (1995). *Releasing the imagination: Essays on education, the arts, and social change.* San Francisco, CA: Jossey-Bass.

Kelchtermans, G. (2005). Teachers' emotions in educational reforms: Self-understanding, vulnerable commitment and micropolitical literacy. *Teaching and Teacher Education, 21*(8), 995–1006.

Keyes, D. (2011). Sunshine and shadows: Opening spaces for creativity, metaphor, and paradox in teaching and teacher education. In C. Craig & L. F. Deretchin (Eds.), *The association of teacher educators (ATE) teacher education yearbook XVII: Cultivating curious and creative minds: The role of teacher education.* Lanham, MD: Scarecrow Education.

Lane, B. (1988). *Landscapes of the sacred: Geography and narrative in American spirituality.* New York, NY: Paulist Press.

Olson, M., & Craig, C. (2005). Uncovering cover stories: Tensions and entailments in the development of teacher knowledge. *Curriculum Inquiry, 35*(2), 161–182.

Olson, M., & Craig, C. (2009a). Traveling stories: Converging milieus and educational conundrums. *Teaching and Teacher Education, 25,* 1077–1085.

Olson, M., & Craig, C. (2009b). Small stories and mega-stories: Accountability in balance. *Teachers College Record, 111*(2), 547–572.

Schön, D. (1983). *The reflective practitioner: How professionals think in action.* New York, NY: Basic Books.

Schwab, J. J. (1983). The practical 4: Something for curriculum professors to do. *Curriculum Inquiry, 13*(3), 239–265.

Schwab, J. J. (2007). *Guide to the Joseph J. Schwab papers 1939–1986* (pp. 1–20). Special Collections Research Center, University of Chicago Library. Retrieved from http://ead.lib.uchicago.edu/learn_on3.php?eadid=ICU.SPCL.SCHWABJJ&q=schwab

CHAPTER TWO BRAIDED RIVERS DIALOGUE

Burrowing and Broadening in the Storied Place of Teacher Education

Vicki:

In regard, to uncovering the tension and conceptualizations that come forward in narrative inquiry, I want to bring forward in this interim how we create, then analyze our own field texts in order to think of our teacher educator identities. Candace, the coauthor of Chapter Five, shared with the editors a response to the braided river metaphor which guided the development of this book. I would like to share her writing and respond to it. She wrote:

> *The metaphor, as written, is so beautifully and fluidly depicted. I reacted to it in so many ways. Observing the birds at the braided rivers sounded like an empowering yet, surprisingly, an extremely isolating experience. The site of these rivers converging together accurately reflects how meaning-making is done and how multiple layers of meaning-making unfold over the course of a study, and beyond the artificial confines at the conclusion of a study (as depicted by the river's continued course beyond the line of sight?). I am reminded when thinking about the braided rivers of the starting point of the rivers. I imagine one droplet of water building upon another. Each one tentative and weak on their own, but combining to eventually form powerful rivers that gain momentum and energy as they twist together with new rivers. This seems metaphorical for narrative inquiry, as well as for the community of narrative inquirers. Your own positioning as "sisters" of the braided river brings to mind the inherent or historical "femaleness" of narrative as an expressive form while conveying a sense of kinship and resonance among narrative inquirers and the work that we do. This metaphor reminds me of Xin Li's (2002) concept of Chinese knots and Ming Fang He's (2003) notion of a river forever flowing to bring to light issues of culture and transformation. Thank you for this beautiful metaphor!*

As is Candace, I am struck, too, by the power and feeling of isolation that the image conjures for me. From my own experience, I find writing to be a lonely undertaking. I am glad that Candace recognized this aspect of the meaning-making process in narrative research. There is a fluid nature to it, as hinted at by many in this field, by their references to feelings of uncertainty, murkiness, and finding one's way. As well, there is isolation and connection playing in turns. I felt the sense of kinship in this metaphor, and keenly in the process of putting together this book. This metaphor hints at the interconnections between us all. As I turn my attention in this interim section to the writing of two "sisters" in my narrative family, I find deep and abiding connections with their thinking and writing.

In this chapter, Keyes and Craig present a thoughtful exploration of the narrative dimension of place. Elsewhere in this book, the centrality of place in shaping experience is discussed, intertwining through each chapter. I pull forward in this interim section the notion of the powerful sculpting hands that place has on the creation of identity. I wrote once about never feeling as sure-footed in my self as when I am in Wyoming. It is a place that figures prominently in my development of a sense of who I am. This sentiment echoed in me as I wrote with Shaun and Janice about the dimension of temporality. I address in this interim piece an idea related to betrayal, raised in discussion about Cheryl and Dixie's chapter. It has been stated that one does not really know a place until one has experienced betrayal there. In the discussion, this idea was linked to the experiences of African American members of North American society and slavery, and with Native Americans and the loss of their lands. This chapter prompts me to wander through my sense of self and the way place has impacted who I am. Do I know the place of my growing years because of betrayal? I don't really think so.

Then, again, there is a place I can see from the interstate between Buffalo and Sheridan that is a place with powerful meaning for me. I look across the rolling hills of the foothills of the Big Horn Mountains and know that that is where my brother died. It is a place I don't tread on lightly. I think that there must be places like this for everyone. Imagine if you were connected to someone on a battlefield or the site of a natural disaster. When I was working in Grand Forks, North Dakota, I found when meeting someone for the first time, oftentimes, one of the early things a person needed to share was his or her flood story. The flood in 1997 was an event that shaped everyone in that place.

Even so, I believe place shapes us whether or not we find betrayal. As I consider the places shared in this chapter, I see Dixie in the conference boardroom where she, as a beginning faculty member, was being shaped. I hear her voice, and her silence, in the elevator where she was likewise being shaped. I think about Cheryl's holding so many places at once. I hold these vignettes in relation to a sense of what betrayal means to me. In some instances, I certainly see that betrayal plays a role in shaping identity through place. But, there are other elements at play. I see vulnerability in the mix as well between place and identity. Vulnerability because, in being shaped, we're learning – learning who we are – learning how to be – stepping into a learning position makes us vulnerable – unsure – uncertain – and dependent on those around us. I remind myself of this vulnerability in my interactions with my preservice teachers as they move into schools.

In addition to the thoughtful ways that place is explored in this chapter, another aspect that I highlight in this interim writing is the tracing tool that Keyes presents in her writing. In terms of narrative methodology, I find this tool extremely helpful. The possibilities that could arise between tracings, in a literary/language arts-based sense, and visual arts tools would be interesting to explore. Certainly, there is methodological merit to playing with this notion in relation to graphic arts novels/work.

Related to Craig's writing for this chapter, I wanted to highlight her interpretive work as she moved through various places and followed interconnected themes of grand narratives in education. She followed the trail of gender in teacher education across time and place, and she portrayed the changing story of teacher education. Her broadening work played a harmonious counterpoint to the burrowing that Keyes provided in this chapter.

Dixie:
Vicki, I, too, resonated with Candace's imagistic response to the embodied braided rivers, especially when she described the droplets of water building on one another until powerful rivers are formed. This image almost perfectly describes the "shaping" you mention. I *felt* this throughout the entire experience writing for the symposium and continuing it with the development of the chapter. I felt the discomfort at having a droplet form over my own, yet simultaneously I felt power from it. And finally, I feel as if Cheryl and I have created a flowing stream that is running into one of the powerful rivers of narrative inquiry.

To add to your interpretation of the notion of betrayal, I did feel as if betrayal helped me to *truly* know my place or places, but this has been a constant for me throughout my life. Through various personal betrayals, I found my resilience and a voice that was stronger *because* of the betrayal. Knowing Cheryl's longitudinal research and writing on school reform which has involved narrative inquiries into crossing boundaries of place (Craig, 2007), I know that she too, has excavated various betrayals on her professional landscape to make sense of and advocate for reform in several educational and professional contexts. I suppose that because of betrayal found in place, I sometimes lack the lens through which I can see and value the beauty, the warmth, or the inspiration I crave. Here I go with vulnerability again, but that said, narrative inquiry and the three-dimensional inquiry space are a home for me, and living within and with you and others joining me, I find the future.

Elaine:
Related to Vicki's notion of the interconnections between place and identity, and more specifically, how people from a commonplace often refer back to a shared event as a means of grounding their identity to that place, I thought about ways in which a place may conjure images of events that had occurred in these places, and how even decades later, may continue to have an impact on those for whom powerful memories are associated with that particular place. I thought of Vicki at the place off the highway where her brother died. I thought of Dixie in the elevator where she listened to, and stewed about, what was being said about teachers but did not feel she could defend herself or those she represented from the attack. I thought about the vulnerability that Dixie likely felt as she interacted but did not agree with ideas expressed by more experienced colleagues. I thought about Cheryl in meetings with colleagues who spoke about the "golden years" in education that were no longer. I thought about my grandparents, and in particular, to my Grandfather, and his experiences as someone who fled his home, the place so influential in shaping his identity, in order to avoid political persecution.

Throughout my childhood, I remember scoffing at the "older generation" of aunts, uncles, and grandparents who had lived through the spread of Communist rule in China before leaving to establish new homes and settle in communities in North America. I could not understand the impact of this event yet knew that it was powerful from the response of those who spoke about it whenever they were in the presence of others they knew had also lived the experience. Their memories of a place – their childhood homes and lives – were so significantly shaped by these events that they were pivotal to their sense of being Chinese in North America. Their departures from their home countries did indeed involve betrayal – of family members, neighbors, acquaintances who seemed to show a willingness to denounce non believers, sometimes to reinforce perceptions of their own strong affiliations to those in power. Yet despite the obvious negative experiences associated with accusations of political wrongdoing and subsequent immigration and resettlement in North America, talk of the spread of Communism in China and later, the Cultural Revolution, remain a point of connection for many Chinese in North American communities. Was it affiliation by association to these events in China that reinforced these connections? I am uncertain but do know that mention of the spread of Communism by my student participant presented in the Chan and Schlein chapter (later in this book) was a point of connection between my student participant and myself, despite the fact that neither of us were born in China nor had spent much time (if any, in my case) there, and were born years after these political events had taken place. We seemed to feel a connection to a place that had contributed to shaping a sense of cultural identity, even if only by association of our ethnic communities.

As I read Vicki's writing about the possible meaning of betrayal in deepening our understanding of a place, and alternatively, the possible alternative interpretation of the idea of betrayal as vulnerability instead, I thought about the moments of connections when we do not quite know how to respond, such as when someone has shared with us something deep and important to their sense of identity. Who we are as teachers and teacher educators are shaped by so many factors that it is at times difficult to acknowledge appropriately the many ways in which our professional knowledge may be shaped by personal and professional experiences lived along the way.

I thought of the stories Dixie and Cheryl shared in this chapter as being among those stories where the teachers and teacher educators shared parts of their histories that have contributed to shaping their sense of professional identity, and know that regardless of whether we are open and/or willing to talk about these instances that reveal our vulnerabilities, that likely, they are a powerful influence in shaping who we are. In the process of sharing these experiences with others, we may worry about opening ourselves up to criticism. At the same time, these stories are powerful for their potential to bridge distances among professionals. In the process of sharing the stories, we are revealing vulnerabilities and opening up the conversation to a further sharing of vulnerabilities among those with whom we are conversing. These vulnerabilities offer a glimpse of the kinds of experiences that motivate a commitment to teaching, especially during difficult times of intense public scrutiny and adherence to standardization and testing in teaching that go beyond what we may believe to be beneficial to student learning. It is these stories that provide us with a glimpse of the reasons for which teachers may continue to teach in spite of difficult professional circumstances.

I thought about whether examining these stories might offer us insight into reasons for which teachers stay with teaching when so many others choose to leave the profession after a short number of years in the field. The field of education, and more specifically, the work of teacher educators within this field, is without doubt, laden with instances when the judgment of one may be caste in doubt when confronted with those who hold ideas vastly different from our own. Having the space to explore these interactions and to reflect upon their impact in shaping a sense of identity, is a powerful professional, and personal, experience.

REFERENCES

Craig, C. (2007, October). Dilemmas in crossing the boundaries. *Teaching and Teacher Education, 23*(7), 1165–1176.

He, M. F. (2003). *A river forever flowing: Cross-cultural lives and identities in the multicultural landscape.* Greenwich, CT: Information Age.

Li, X. (2002). *The Tao of life stories: Chinese language, poetry, and culture in education.* New York, NY: Peter Lang.

CHAPTER THREE

ATTENDING TO THE TEMPORAL DIMENSION OF NARRATIVE INQUIRY INTO TEACHER EDUCATOR IDENTITIES

M. Shaun Murphy, Vicki Ross and Janice Huber

ABSTRACT

Purpose – *The purpose of this chapter is to explore and make visible narrative thinking as an interpretive act in moving from field texts to research texts.*

Approach – *The chapter shows a collaborative meaning-making process of three teacher educators/researchers as they inquire into their identities as teacher educators. The chapter is framed around a focus on temporality, one commonplace within the three-dimensional narrative inquiry space and also shows connections with the two other commonplaces of sociality and place.*

Findings – *The researchers deepen the understanding of identity as situated in a continuity of experience in relation with others. They highlight how stories beget a storied response. They demonstrate that the experiential dimensions of sociality, temporality, and spatiality are interconnected. They find, through thinking narratively, that the relational* is critical – both historically and in the present. *Relationships shape a sense of self.* This relational aspect of their research introduces ethical considerations. It is in honoring the stories they carry and the stories that are given to or shared with them that the possibility exists for shaping a responsive and attentive life.

Research implications – *Numerous authors have written about the relational aspects of narrative inquiry as a research methodology. This chapter shows ways in which the relational aspects of narrative inquiry shaped both our inquiry into and our understandings of our identities as teacher educators. These foundational aspects of the relational both in terms of narrative inquiry as a research methodology and in identity inquiry open up many future research possibilities which extend far beyond narrative inquiry into teacher educator identity.*

Value – *Researchers utilizing a narrative inquiry approach will find a helpful explanation and demonstration of the process of making meaning of field texts by situating them within the three-dimensional narrative inquiry space.*

Keywords: Narrative inquiry; temporality; identity; relational ethics; three-dimensional narrative inquiry space

BEGINNING IN EXPERIENCE

I was a grade six boy in Mrs. T's room. In our classroom were two sisters in the same grade. Noreen and Alene[1] were Aboriginal girls who lived somewhere in town, somewhere I did not know. In class they were silent, they talked with no one but each other, and, when they did, they talked quietly.

On the day I am recalling, my brothers and I were late for school, again. It was a cold winter day. We had piled into the blue station wagon for our father to drive us to school from our farm in the country. As we got close to the school, we saw Noreen and Alene walking. My father slowed to pick them up. He knew them from his work as a social worker in town and, conversely, this meant they knew him.

"What are you doing, Dad?" I asked.

"Stopping to pick them up."

We were close enough to the school that they would not have had much more to walk, but far enough that a car ride would make a difference, plus it was cold.

"They're almost there," I spoke out.

They were almost there, why bother stopping, the car was full with six of us, we were already late, all reasons to keep driving, all reasons I could have said out loud except for the real one. I didn't want to be seen arriving at school with them.

My father looked at me and frowned a little, "It's cold Shaun, and we're stopping to pick them up."

And so we did. The car pulled up beside them, and my father called for them to get in. Shyly they did, giggling and smiling, and my father pulled away from the curb and drove the rest of the short distance to the school. Already I was strategizing – "How could I get into class without anyone knowing we had given them a lift?" Here my memory ends. I recall nothing else of the day.

Janice's Written Response	*Vicki's Written Response*
On the day in mid-December when we were scheduled to talk about our paper, it was long before sunrise when I first sat at my desk quietly reading Shaun's story. As I read Shaun's story, once, twice, and then a third time, I became increasingly drawn toward Noreen and Alene, two girls of Aboriginal ancestry whom Shaun described as living "on the margins" of his life and also, from Shaun's perspective, on the margins of the life of the classroom and the small rural town where they were situated. Did Noreen and Alene complete school, I wondered. Do they still live in this community? Do their children now attend this school? Were Noreen and Alene still alive? As this last question lingered, I was suddenly drawn backward in time to memories lived in another school place:	Marginalization There is a picture that immediately jumps into my mind as I read Shaun's story – it is an image of my second-grade-self standing at the old-fashioned wrought-iron fence that ringed the elementary schoolyard block in my hometown. I had run to the fence to greet .... *Well, let me explain – my father's Uncle Harry was the town drunk. Alcohol and its use and abuse weave their way through much of my childhood memories.* *Uncle Harry had a pile of children, only three of whom I knew growing up: Charlie (who was my younger brother's age), Maude (who was in my class when my family moved back to Buffalo, Wyoming), and Doris (who was older than me by five years). These children lived in*

Gina
Friends
We played together
Every day
Her home, my home
We were inseparable

Began grade one
Still early in the year
We stood in the hallway
A long line of children

Silent, we waited to enter a doorway
Into a room with little light
It was dusty, cluttered with cans, rags, and buckets
Teachers were talking, laughing
Around us, above us
As each child moved
To the front of the line
Their hair was checked

Gina was ahead of me
"She has them," said the teachers
And they whisked her away to a sink in the corner

It was large, gray, and metal
A teacher poured something smelly
Onto Gina's head
Another teacher scrubbed
Roughly
The line moved forward
I returned to the hallway
Where the grade one children
Stood
In single file

a shack next door to the James'. In small town Buffalo, Wyoming, the James family lived on the fringes of town, figuratively not literally. They were poor, very poor.

...I had run to the fence to say hello to Doris and her next-door friend who were walking down Fort Street to school, not recognizing the social cost, determined by the other children in town, of this connection I was so openly making ... .

Here is the way my tensions – unimagined yet by my open and loving second-grade self – were embraced by my mother. She recognized early the social jeopardy I would be in. The following week, she shimmied into her cream-colored, mohair sweater dress and her fur coat, slipped on her open-toed, "don't mess with me" heels, and her sassy attitude, and paid a classroom visit. As she entered my new world, I remember the beauty, confidence, and grace that she brought with her. She came to volunteer to be our classroom parent coordinator.

Although she died decades ago, my mother is, even still, a force to be reckoned with in my life.

Another threaded memory of this resonating image is another image ... .

Attending to the Temporal Dimension of Narrative Inquiry

Silent
Waiting
For Gina
Whose soft cries
Echoed
From the end of the line
As we eventually
Walked
Slowly back to the grade one classroom

I was scared
I wanted to go home

As Greene (1995) writes, "clearly, we cannot return to the landscapes" of our childhoods; "we can only become present to them by reflecting on them" (p. 73). And, so, it was in my present thinking with Shaun's story that I felt myself shifting through memory over 40 years back in time and place to thoughts of Gina. As my above memory fragments show, Gina and I were friends as two young girls whose lives met outside of school. Our play together was threaded by hours outside where our imaginations guided us. Sometimes we played on the steps of one of our homes, other times we ventured into the trees and tall grass, eventually making our way to the nearby creek or barn. As we entered grade one the freedom of our play and friendship changed. I do not recall a lot about grade one, other than the

My mother is standing in the kitchen of the home in which Charlie, Maude, and Doris grew up. Uncle Harry's wife "took in" ironing to make ends meet – or, I suspect now as an adult, to bring them a little closer together because the ends probably seldom met. When picking up our ironing, Mom had found out that Maude's birthday was that day, and it was going uncelebrated. My mother picked up my younger brother, Billy, and I from school. We went to J.C. Penney's and bought a stocking cap (a fashion-statement all those years ago) and a matching pair of mittens. We wrapped them and off we went.

The image I carry in my heart is of my mother standing in the unfamiliar kitchen stirring by hand a bowl of chocolate cake batter. My mother was baking a birthday cake for Maude. She had never had a birthday cake ... .

The troubled storyline I went on to live with Maude throughout my childhood is not one that sits easily with me as an adult, as a teacher, or as a teacher of teachers. It is one of social self-preservation and the guilt that comes with that. But, the touchstone is feelings of shame, loneliness, and longing *that shade in the image of that second-grade girl standing at the fence.* (Vicki's story shared in response to Shaun's story, Winter, 2011) foreboding silence, loneliness, and fear I felt and one or two memories of children whose experiences caused me to beg my parents to let me stay home. My memory of Gina's experience in the janitor's room is one of these few memories.

I remember, too, Gina's mom's tears at the end of that school day, and at the end of many school days. Gina and her family moved back to the nearby reservation soon after we began grade one. I never saw Gina again. Many years later, just weeks before I completed a B.Ed. degree, my mom called to tell me that Gina had been killed. She had been heading home, walking along the edge of the highway and was hit by a truck. (Janice's story shared in response to Shaun's story, Winter, 2011)

We begin our chapter with these three stories of experience, each represented in differing font, as they initiated our narrative inquiry into the temporal aspects of our identities as teacher educators. As shown above, our narrative inquiry began with Shaun's story, to which Janice and Vicki each responded. Much has happened since we first wrote, shared, and began to inquire into our above stories. Because we live at a physical distance from one another, our narrative inquiry has unfolded though our ongoing conversations via SKYPE, the telephone, and e-mail. Indeed, it was living through our narrative inquiry in this way, as a kind of sustained, although shifting and evolving conversation, that shaped our decision to represent our chapter as a conversation. As we gradually decided to represent our chapter as a conversation we drew upon earlier work in which we created a "fictionalized" account as our research text: "In constructing these research texts ... we changed the order of the conversation, placed different pieces of text in new juxtapositions, assigned speakers' names and composed what we hope is a telling research text" (Steeves et al., 2009, p. 58). This chapter was shaped in similar ways so as to represent a multi-voiced, although fictionalized, conversation. As well, because our narrative inquiry did not follow a linear, step-by-step formula but moved in multiple directions while circling around reverberating ideas so, too, does the conversation that we created as a way to represent our chapter.

As in the living out of our narrative inquiry the first direction in which our chapter moves is toward our need, as narrative inquirers, to think narratively. We then engage in thinking narratively in relation with our experiences storied at the chapter's beginning. Since our engagement in thinking narratively brought more sharply into focus the temporal dimensions of our lived and told stories of experience, our chapter also turns toward a discussion of this. The subsequent section shows the complexity we experienced in the midst of our narrative inquiry as we metaphorically brought our earlier understandings, shaped through thinking narratively, alongside our understandings of the continuity and temporality of experience. These notions of the centrality of the relational nature of narrative inquiry drew our attention to ways in which this relational aspect is entwined with the temporal qualities of experience. As a result, our chapter also moves in this direction. The final path taken in our conversation is toward insights gained through our narrative inquiry into our identities as teacher educators, particularly through attentiveness to the entangled temporal and relational dimensions of who we are and who we are becoming.

THINKING NARRATIVELY AS NARRATIVE INQUIRERS

Shaun: When I think narratively about our three stories I am guided by Connelly and Clandinin's (1990) understanding that "narrative is both phenomenon and method":

> ... narrative names the structured quality of experience to be studied, and it names the patterns of inquiry for its study. ... Thus, we say that people by nature lead storied lives and tell stories of those lives, whereas narrative researchers describe such lives, collect and tell stories of them, and write narratives of experience. (p. 2)

Janice: Clandinin and Connelly's (2000) understanding of narrative as both phenomenon and method in narrative inquiry encourages me, as a narrative inquirer, to not lose sight of experience as I engage in

Vicki: narrative inquiries, living through each phase of the inquiry: living in the field and composing field texts and then as I inquire into the field texts and compose interim and research texts.

Vicki: I think Clandinin and Connelly (2000)'s term, "thinking narratively" names this sustained attention to understanding experience narratively. Thinking narratively is thinking within a metaphorical "three-dimensional narrative inquiry space" (p. 49).

Shaun: Clandinin and Connelly's description of the three dimensions of this space or the three "commonplaces of narrative inquiry" (Connelly & Clandinin, 2006) are:

> ... personal and social (interaction); past, present, and future (continuity): combined with the notion of place (situation). This set of terms creates a metaphorical three-dimensional narrative inquiry space, with temporality along one dimension, the personal and social along a second dimension, and place along a third. Using this set of terms, any particular inquiry is defined by this three-dimensional space: studies have temporal dimensions and address temporal matters; they focus on the personal and social in a balance appropriate to the inquiry; and they occur in specific places or sequences of places. (Clandinin & Connelly, 2000, p. 50)

Janice: Thinking narratively, attending to the temporal, social, and place dimensions of our stories of experience is a way to stay acutely attentive to lives for "narrative inquiry is about life and living" (Connelly & Clandinin, 2006, p. 478). Indeed, "what makes a narrative inquiry is the simultaneous exploration of all three" (p. 479) of the dimensions or commonplaces of experience and the resulting stories lived and told[2].

Vicki: This means, then, that while our focus in this chapter is on the temporal nature of experience, we understand that who we are and who we are *temporally* becoming is also shaped through social and place interactions.

Thinking Narratively With Our Stories

Shaun: The story I shared of Alene and Noreen is one I always carry with me, and it seems to come up again and again since I have started living in the world of teacher education. I remember first writing about it in 2000 for a writing project tied to an earlier grant. The version here is the latest iteration. I have to admit I have never told the story to my undergraduate classes of preservice teachers. I did once tell it in a graduate class. Afterwards, there was silence.

I broke the silence that day as led a discussion into what the story was saying to me. There are so many layers to this story.

It is interesting to me that when we were first approached to write about temporality – and as a group we decided to write stories – that this is the one I wrote. This is not the story that I pull out for talks about temporality; in fact, I have never tried to think of one of the narrative commonplaces (Connelly & Clandinin, 2006) separately from the others. Even now, I cannot think about this story without considering the other people in it and the places where it occurred. However, this story is most certainly located in time. It has a past in that, when I was a young boy, it did occur; it has a present in that I think often about what it means for me now; and, I know it has a shaping influence on my future.

My understanding of temporality is based on the writings of Clandinin and Connelly (1995, 1996, 2000) and Connelly and Clandinin (2006). It is also influenced by Dewey's (1938) notion of continuity, in that each experience builds on or is shaped by previous ones. In part, who I am, today, is built upon that moment in the car because my identity is constructed from so many other experiences: experiences with my dad, experiences with my grade six teacher, the other children in the class, and a memory of Alene and Noreen in that grade six classroom. My focus on this narrative moment now positions it more influentially in my present. Once, when I mentioned it to my dad, he had no memory of this moment at all. Nor, I suspect, would any of the other people in it. However, I pull this memory forward to remind myself of the importance of what children negotiate, mostly silently, in classrooms, and how teachers have to make space and be acutely aware of the webs of relationships and non-relationships that exist in classrooms.

What is clear to me in this story is that it is a story about relationship. Primarily it is about the relationship between the Shaun of now and the young Shaun of the past. It is about the lack of relationship between Alene, Noreen, and Shaun. While there *was* a lack of relationship in our elementary classroom, I have maintained one with them for a long time since. It is about a son and his Dad, a school boy and his teacher, and that same school boy and his peers. All of these people reach out from the past and, in a sense, have an expectation of attention. I have an obligation to all of these people, and I live out this obligation in the context of my work in teacher education.

Vicki: Shaun, when I responded to your story, the hook into my past was the children who are treated as outcasts, those ones who are marginalized by their classmates and by society. For me, this was my cousin. But, your story also contained the parent figure who was trying to help you learn how to be in the world: how to treat people and how to be the person who reaches out. That's the connection for me with my mother. She was also teaching me life lessons: the importance of kindness, generosity, and strength of character. Many of the lessons I learned about being a teacher and about my identity as a teacher, mother, and teacher educator are ones that I learned with and through her.

Ultimately, Shaun, your story captured for me a story of loss and remembrance, perhaps a continuing grieving I do and perhaps you do as well, for your missing parent. Just a thought ....

Shaun: I wonder if telling this story is about the obligation involved in it. Can one have temporal obligations? By that, I mean obligations to persons who do not people your present. Although, I used this story to initiate our work on temporality, its deeper resonance resides in the relational.

Vicki: When you talk about obligations, I am reminded of a recent conversation I had with my stepmother about the memory I shared with you and Janice. You speak of obligation to your younger self and persons who do not people your present. That is certainly the case for family obligations ... individuals who had such a shaping influence in your youth and who are gone or passed away from your present. How, then, do we write of these experiences? They are so foundational to a sense of self, they're constructed with characters for whom you have a sense of responsibility and obligation, yet, your truth may not represent their truth. There are no easy or simple answers to these research questions.

Janice: As I wrote in response to your story, one complexity that emerged for me, as a result of my responding with my story of Gina and of our experiences prior to and as we began grade one, is that this is not a story I previously connected with my gradual decision to become a teacher. There are, actually, experiences that have always been acutely central in my becoming a teacher – experiences I lived over many years as a child and youth alongside my youngest brother and the daily humiliation and punishment that shaped his journey in the rural northern Alberta school we attended. My brother differed in many ways from the students who attended this school and whose presence there, day-after-day, seemed much more valued. Nothing about my brother ever seemed valued, especially not his differing ways of knowing or of showing what he knew. In loving him, I felt, at least in some small way, the daily pain he endured.

All through our narrative inquiry I have felt that if I had sat down to write a story into which I, and we, might have inquired as a way to understand something more about who I am and who I am becoming as a teacher educator, I likely would have written of a moment of tension lived in a recent teacher education classroom or of my brother or maybe even of my living as a mother alongside my young daughter as she now navigates life in school. However, none of these experiences were foregrounded as I read, multiple times, your story, Shaun. Instead, what your story elicited in me was an intense calling. The intense calling I experienced was shaped through my many questions about Noreen and Alene. I was not once drawn toward questions of Shaun, nor of Shaun's dad or his siblings nor to other experiences lived in his life. My attention was solely sustained on Noreen and Alene as I wondered about their experiences, both in that long-ago time, place, situation, and relationships and in more present times, places, situations, and relationships.

What my puzzling here awakens me to is nothing new, which is the deeply relational nature of experience, stories, and narrative inquiry (Clandinin & Connelly, 2000; Connelly & Clandinin, 1990; Craig & Huber, 2007). For me, the space shaped in this meeting of our stories of experience was filled with wonderings about lives, past, present, and future. For example, in thinking about a commonality in both Shaun's and my stories in relation with Noreen's, Alene's, and Gina's lives in school, in this moment, I *wished* I had lived differently with Gina in grade one. And, as I reflected on this grade one experience, today, as a teacher educator, I wondered what had changed. Time certainly has passed and, although I know much more today than I did in grade one about the colonization of Aboriginal people in Canada and elsewhere (Battiste, 2004; Grant, 2004; Royal Commission on Aboriginal Peoples, 1996; Smith, 1999), knowing that the post-secondary education gap continues to grow between Aboriginal and non-Aboriginal people in Canada (Canadian Council on Learning, 2009), I wonder. What has changed?

PUZZLING OVER EXPERIENCE

Vicki: As I think about some of what we seem to be puzzling over in our inquiry into our stories, I am reminded of Dewey and, in particular, this idea:

> The statement that individuals live in a world means, in the concrete, that they live in a series of situations ... .interaction is going on between an individual and objects and other persons. The conceptions of *situation* and *interaction* are inseparable from each other. An experience is always what it is because of a transaction taking place between an individual and what, at the time, constitutes his environment ... (Dewey, 1938, p. 41)

Janice: It is very helpful to be reminded of Dewey's criteria of experience as we take the initial steps in a process of making more transparent our meaning-making in relation with our field texts and our stories of experience.

Shaun: Yes, drawing upon Dewey's terms to think through the stages of our interpretive acts, positions situations and interactions as the constituents of an experience. These two concepts are integral to one another, much the way that the narrative dimensions or commonplaces of temporality, sociality, and place twine together: they exist in relation to one another.

Vicki: The situation we inquired into, then, was a story of an experience Shaun recalled from his childhood. But, there was a duality of situation in our shared narrative inquiry in that, while we explored Shaun's experience, we also entered into a situation as researchers. We come together to an experience in the present. Situations are made up of, what Dewey (1938) calls, "external conditions" (p. 27), or contextualizing factors of an experience, and "internal conditions," which refer more to the sense of self that an individual pulls into a situation.

Janice: This sense of self is constructed along a temporal continuum, what is called a "continuity of experience." Dewey (1938) posited that this continuity of experience, " ... covers the formation of attitudes, attitudes that are emotional and intellectual; it covers our basic sensitivities and ways of meeting and responding to all the conditions which we meet in living" (p. 27). Shaun brought into our narrative inquiry space one storied fragment of his "continuity of experience" and, thus, set in motion our inquiry into his story.

Shaun: So, Janice, in your response to my story, you then found yourself sharing a story from your childhood. Do you see what I mean? Your internal conditions were elicited by my story. In this way, you connected a story of your experience through and in your life, to interpret my story. Vicki, you also did this.

Vicki: Um hum, we entered into an "experience" in that, in our present situation, each one of us brought a continuity of experience that interacted with the others' continuities of experience. The experience, made up in this situation and interaction, made possible new understandings. For example, both of you, Shaun and Janice, had an opportunity in which to grow, which, in Dewey's (1938) terms, is an "educative" (p. 25) experience.

Janice: And, similarly, Vicki, as you entered into Shaun's remembrance you found yourself encountering a scene from your childhood.

Shaun: As we have been dwelling in this Deweyan notion of experience, two important thoughts arise. The first is that our narrative inquiry is into my experience. Each of your stories, Janice and Vicki, were called forth from your continuities and shared in response to my story. Secondly, it is important to note that you responded to my story with a story; you were thinking narratively and responded narratively as a form of inquiry.

Vicki: Yes, we are thinking through story. The three of us did not independently write stories to share with one another, nor did Janice and I respond to each other's stories. What I hope we can think more about is this responsive quality of our storytelling. Can we think more, together, about how this layering of stories is, in itself, an analytic act? Because we human beings are meaning-makers and seek points of connection between ourselves and others, the layering of stories seems to be one way we do this.

Janice: As I think about what you are saying about the "responsive quality of our storytelling," Vicki, I am reminded of how Coles (1989) described this embodied draw or tug that we experience in relation with stories as "the call of stories." Do you remember Coles' story of his meetings and learning alongside Dr. Ludwig, one of his supervisors during his residency as a beginning psychiatrist? He stories these experiences with Dr. Ludwig as

> profoundly shaping his learning about the importance and power of stories.

Shaun: I have *The Call of Stories* (Coles, 1989) right here so I will read some of this while we are on SKYPE:

> Dr. Ludwig saw me at eight, before he saw his patients, and there were days when I felt like one of them – I had very little to report, so I felt apprehensive: all those minutes, with at best contrived talk. The doctor across the room took quick stock of the situation and told me *he* wanted a little time that morning, if it was all right with me. He announced that he was going to tell me a "story." My ears perked up. ... Dr. Ludwig's story concerned a patient, a woman almost paralyzed by various worries and fears. The doctor told me a very great deal about her ... most of all, the *events* in her life: where she met her husband and how, where she traveled and why, where she spent her spare time and with whom. I was quite taken up by listening. ... Suddenly the story stopped: the patient had been struck by a car, on the way to a lecture at an art museum. I was surprised, saddened. I felt questions welling up in me. What happened to her as a result of the injuries she sustained, and in general, as she got older? ... Dr. Ludwig suddenly stopped to think ... he sat and looked at me. I wondered why, what to say, to ask. The silence was broken by his question: "Do you see her in your mind?" "Yes," I answered. "Good," he responded. ... "I have told you a story," the doctor said. Nothing more. I awaited an amplification in vain. It was my turn. I responded to the storyteller, not the doctor, the psychiatrist, the supervisor: "What happened?" I was a little embarrassed at the sound in my own ears of those two words, for I felt I ought to have asked a shrewd psychological question. But Dr. Ludwig said he was glad I'd asked the question I did. Then he told me "what happened." Afterward there was a different kind of silence in the room, for I was thinking about what I'd heard, and he was remembering what he had experienced. (pp. 6–7)

Vicki: It is interesting to think about how we, too, both responded to Shaun, the storyteller. Neither of us responded to Shaun, the doctor, or to Shaun, the teacher educator, or to Shaun, the friend. In many ways we each, because we also traveled backward in time and place as we responded, responded to Shaun, the 11-year-old boy whose living all those years ago called forward aspects of each of our own much earlier lives.

Janice: And, similar to what Coles experienced at the end of Dr. Ludwig's story, Vicki, our responses also seem threaded by questions of "what happened?" While neither of us specifically asked this question of Shaun in either of our responses, we did each kind of puzzle over this question within the context of our own lived experiences, which were called forward in relation with Shaun's story.

Shaun: Acknowledging this inward–outward process as an act of analysis turns my thinking back to Dewey's criteria of experience. There were certain conditions of the "situation" that shaped this creation of connections between us, as individuals.

Vicki: In our case, the relational aspects of our inquiry were essential, allowing us to share stories in which we felt vulnerable, thus, enabling us to work toward the reconstruction of these experiences – a restorying of our lives, an opportunity for growth, a realization of a truly educative moment.

Janice: I think this is the hope of narrative inquiry which Clandinin and Rosiek (2007), wrote about:

> Dewey's (1981c) conception of experience ... is a changing stream that is characterized by continuous interaction of human thought with our personal, social, and material environment .... [This] implies that the regulative ideal for inquiry is not to generate an exclusively faithful representation of a reality independent of the knower. The regulative ideal for inquiry is to generate a new relation between a human being and her environment – her life, community, world – one that "makes possible a new way of dealing with them, and thus eventually creates a new kind of experienced objects, not more real than those which preceded but more significant, and less overwhelming and oppressive" (Dewey, 1981b, p. 175). In this pragmatic view of knowledge, our representations arise from experience and must return to that experience for their validation. (p. 39)

Attending to the Interweaving of the Temporal and the Relational in Composing Lives as Teacher Educators

Shaun: It's been good to revisit Dewey's (1938) continuity of experience because the narrative dimension with which we are concerned in this chapter is temporality. In narrative inquiry, temporality is a central concept which Clandinin and Connelly (2000) developed through studying Dewey's work. They remind us that this temporal dimension of narrative inquiry relates to the existential nature of experience; life happens in a very real present. When we consider the temporal nature of experience, we see, also, how life happens over time. Our past experiences, and how we have made sense of them, shape our present experiences, and how we understand them. In narrative inquiry, Clandinin and Connelly (2000) remind us that "experience is temporal" and also, that "experiences taken collectively are temporal" (p. 19).

Vicki: These notions of temporality within narrative inquiry, as put forward by Clandinin and Connelly (2000), are organically related to Dewey's notion of the continuity of experience (1938). What we know, really, who we are, is the sum of our experiences and the meaning we made, make, and are remaking of them. In this way, then, our biographical histories, our pasts, shape our presents, and together they move us into our futures (Connelly & Clandinin, 1988).

Janice: I have a strong sense of this linking, and remaking, of our past, present, and future experiences as I linger with my earlier questions about how the lives of Aboriginal people weave into my teaching and living in teacher education classrooms. For example, I wonder if my interactions with pre-service teachers encourage them to live with Aboriginal children and families in ways in which the grade one teachers in my storied memory lived with Gina. And, as I interact with Aboriginal teachers in a teacher education program, am I, as Gina's and my grade one teachers may have been, being shaped by an unbroken institutional narrative that, as a non-Aboriginal person, I know what is best and have the right to impose my beliefs and ways onto the Aboriginal students with whom I work?

Shaun: Another aspect to which we attended, while thinking temporally about our stories of experience, was the way in which social contexts interacted with our personal experiences. Not only do an individual's experiences happen within a continuity, so, too, do the contexts in which those experiences happen. What I think we each felt, and tried to show, was the potential changing nature of social contexts over time.

Vicki: In terms of the temporal nature of narrative inquiry, Clandinin and Connelly explained "we see how life happens in an historical sense as well" (2000, p. 19). As narrative inquirers inquiring into field texts, we are directed to attend to evolving social contexts, "the people, schools, and educational landscapes we study undergo day-by-day experiences that are contextualized within a longer-term historical narrative" (p. 19). In our inquiry at the heart of this narrative study, we see that each of our experiences is set in a very real place, places which hold potential for shifting over time.

Janice: Yes, we saw that the places of each of our childhoods have forward temporality, but carry within them a historical trace of

	earlier attitudes, habits, and beliefs reconstructed with and through present-day experiences.
Shaun:	Something else that seemed to emerge through our earlier inquiry into our stories is the interwoven nature of the temporal and the relational aspects of our experiences. In puzzling over these connections, I am again reminded of Coles (1997), when he wrote that:

> ... the point of personal stories ... is not self-accusation. ... The point is to summon one's frail side so as to enable a more forthright sharing of experiences on the part of all of us: that guy has stumbled, and he's not making too much of it, but he *is* putting it on the table, and thereby I'm enabled to put some of myself, my remembrances, my story, on the table, whether explicitly, by speaking up or, in the way many of us do, by also remembering – another's memories trigger our own. (pp. 11–12)

Vicki:	Shaun's openness in sharing his frail side connected me immediately and powerfully with recollections and stories that I seldom tell others. The relationship I have with Shaun and Janice, and the sense of trust that threads through our relationship, made it possible for me to take a look, again, at these memories. Engaging in a reconstructive moment, I ask myself, from these memories, "What is of most worth for me to pull forward into my teacher educator self?" This growing up – this being human, really, – is messy, messy business. Teaching is living and being in relation with vulnerable others making their way. Be attuned to who they are and are becoming and to who you are and are becoming.
Janice:	Coles' (1997) thoughts deeply resonate with my experiences in the process of our narrative inquiry. I continue to experience dis-ease and discomfort as I remember Gina. However, increasingly, I see the value of my telling and inquiring into the experiences I remember living alongside her. While I have certainly thought of Gina throughout my life, remembering her, again, because of Shaun's story has shifted my childhood sense of fear to a sense of the urgent responsibilities I carry as a teacher educator.
Shaun:	Janice, what you say is so important to me. When I wrote my story it was not to castigate the 11-year-old boy I was all those years ago. My reason was to locate myself temporally in a story that shapes my work in teacher education. When Vicki spoke earlier about the lives of children on the margins, and when

	you wrote about Gina's and your brother's places in school, this attention to the places for children in school is what Alene and Noreen remind me to be attentive to. I hold the wonderings you do, as well, Janice, about the ways our work in teacher education supports pre-service teachers' understandings of ethical obligations. In that sense, I locate myself in a temporal space, situating myself in the continuity of experience as I honor Alene and Noreen by living alongside imagined children and families that the pre-service teachers will encounter.
Vicki:	The tension inherent in bringing forward past experiences that shape imagined futures is living with the understanding that my life is always in the making. This necessary incompleteness (Miller, 1998) is important in that, if I can hold open this space for my teacher educator identity making, then, I can help shape a space for this kind of process in the lives of pre-service teachers. Given that we continue to inquire into these stories from our past and the way they live in our bodies, highlights our continued need for interaction with them. They cease to be just stories by our inquiry into them (Clandinin & Connelly, 1998), and, in the ways that we retell them in our research and reliving (Clandinin & Connelly, 2000), they become educative in our work as teacher educators.

WEAVING OUR THOUGHTS TOGETHER

This conversation situated our inquiry into our teacher educator identities as meaning-making in progress. Our sense of self, like any identity, is situated in a continuity of experience in relation with others. Our initial stories, pulled from our pasts, shape our current practices in teacher education in nested relationships (Lyons, 1990) with lives from our pasts, presents, and futures. Our responses with stories demonstrated how we were thinking narratively; a story often begets a storied response. While we made the temporal aspect of our inquiry more visible, it was evident that this exists alongside the social and alongside place, and that the three can never be truly separate from one another. Experience happens with others in contexts.

The relationality of our lives was a significant part of this inquiry, not only our relationships with each other, but with the persons that people our lives over time. These relationships shaped us, historically, and continue to do so in our present lives. In our conversations, our storied pasts alongside other children shape our work in teacher education today. We named these as ethical obligations. When writing about ethics, Putnam (2004) wrote that he understands ethics as a "system of interrelated concerns, concerns which [he saw] as mutually supporting but also in partial tension" (p. 22). This reminds us of Cole's (1997) words which we included earlier, "[t]he point is to summon one's frail side so as to enable a more forthright sharing of experiences on the part of all of us" (p. 11). This is the tension in ethics: our stories call us to attend to the lives of children, families, and the teachers with whom we work. Situating his ideas in a Deweyan understanding, Putnam went on to write,

> the idea of ethics [is] concerned with the solution of *practical* problems. ... "practical problems" here means simply "problems we encounter in practice," specific and situated problems. ... What is important is that practical problems, unlike the idealized experiments of the philosophers, as typically "messy." (p. 28, italics and quotation marks in original)

Messy is a good word to describe the complex meetings of diverse lives, particularly in relation to an ethical stance. There is no clear path upon which to build an identity; our identities are always in the making. For us, it is in honouring the stories we carry and the stories that are given to or shared with us that the possibility exists for shaping a responsive and attentive life.

NOTES

1. These names are pseudonyms as are the names of other people who become visible in our stories.
2. As we wrote this chapter we always held the relational as central in our inquiry. For us three, narrative inquiry is a highly relational methodology. We understand the relational in terms of the personal. It was our relationships with each other that allowed us to inquire as deeply as we did into these stories we carry. This relational quality is something we bring to our work with participants by living in ethical ways alongside them in the research. We also highlight the relationships among the narrative commonplaces of temporality, sociality, and place. One commonplace cannot be understood without recognition of its connections to the other two.

ACKNOWLEDGMENTS

We wish to gratefully acknowledge the technical assistance we received from Hayley Fenton, Vicki's daughter, in formatting our chapter.

REFERENCES

Battiste, M. (2004, June). Animating sites of postcolonial education: Indigenous knowledge and the humanities. Paper presented at the annual meeting of the Canadian Society for the Study of Education, Winnipeg, Manitoba.
Canadian Council on Learning. (2009). *Post secondary education in Canada: Meeting our needs?* Ottawa, Canada: Canadian Council on Learning.
Clandinin, D. J., & Connelly, F. M. (1995). *Teachers' professional knowledge landscapes.* New York, NY: Teachers College Press.
Clandinin, D. J., & Connelly, F. M. (1996). Teachers' professional knowledge landscapes: Teacher stories, stories of teachers, school stories, stories of schools. *Educational Researcher, 25*(3), 24–30.
Clandinin, D. J., & Connelly, F. M. (1998). Asking questions about telling stories. In C. Kridel (Ed.), *Writing educational biography: Explorations in qualitative research* (pp. 245–253). New York, NY: Garland Publishing, Inc.
Clandinin, D. J., & Connelly, F. M. (2000). *Narrative inquiry: Experience and story in qualitative research.* San Francisco, CA: Jossey-Bass.
Clandinin, D. J., & Rosiek, J. (2007). Mapping a landscape of narrative inquiry: Borderland spaces and tensions. In D. J. Clandinin (Ed.), *Handbook of narrative inquiry: Mapping a methodology* (pp. 35–75). Thousand Oaks, CA: Sage.
Coles, R. (1989). *The call of stories: Teaching and the moral imagination.* Boston, MA: Houghton Mifflin.
Coles, R. (1997). *Doing documentary work.* Don Mills, ON: Oxford University Press.
Connelly, F. M., & Clandinin, D. J. (1988). *Teachers as curriculum planners: Narratives of experience.* New York, NY: Teachers College Press.
Connelly, F. M., & Clandinin, D. J. (1990). Stories of experience and narrative inquiry. *Educational Researcher, 19*(5), 2–14.
Connelly, F. M., & Clandinin, D. J. (2006). Narrative inquiry. In J. Green, S. Camilli & P. B. Elmore (Eds.), *Handbook of complementary methods in education research* (pp. 477–489). Washington, DC: American Educational Research Association.
Craig, C., & Huber, J. (2007). Relational reverberations: Shaping and reshaping narrative inquiries in the midst of storied lives and contexts. In D. J. Clandinin (Ed.), *Handbook of narrative inquiry: Mapping a methodological landscape* (pp. 251–279). New York, NY: Sage.
Dewey, J. (1938). *Experience and education.* New York, NY: Macmillan.
Grant, A. (2004). *Finding my talk: How fourteen Native Canadian women reclaimed their lives after residential school.* Calgary, Canada: Fifth House Books.
Greene, M. (1995). *Releasing the imagination: Essays on education, the arts, and social change.* San Francisco, CA: Jossey-Bass.
Lyons, N. (1990). Dilemmas of knowing: Ethical and epistemological dimensions of teachers' work and development. *Harvard Educational Review, 60*(2), 159–180.
Miller, J. (1998). Autobiography and the necessary incompleteness of teachers' stories. In W. Ayers & J. Miller (Eds.), *A light in dark times: Maxine Greene and the unfinished conversation* (pp. 145–154). New York, NY: Teachers College Press.
Putnam, H. (2004). *Ethics without ontology.* Cambridge, MA: Harvard University Press.
Royal Commission on Aboriginal Peoples. (1996). *Report of the royal commission on aboriginal peoples.* Ottawa, Canada: Canada Communications Group.

Smith, L. T. (1999). *Decolonizing methodologies: Research and Indigenous peoples*. New York, NY: Zed Books Ltd..

Steeves, P., Pearce, M., Murray Orr, A., Murphy, S. M., Huber, M., Huber, J., & Clandinin, D. J. (2009). What we know first: Interrupting the institutional narrative of individualism. In W. S. Gershon (Ed.), *The collaborative turn: Working together in qualitative research* (pp. 55–69). Rotterdam: Sense Publishers.

CHAPTER THREE BRAIDED RIVERS DIALOGUE

Attending to the Temporal Dimension of Narrative Inquiry into Teacher Educator Identities

Elaine:
Reading this chapter highlighted for me many aspects of building research relationships that parallel the building of relationships with others beyond a research setting – such as with friends, colleagues, and family members. To begin with, I was struck by the power of the role of relationship in shaping the kinds of stories of "very close to the heart" experiences that could be shared and examined. Shaun's story about his memories of interaction with sixth grade classmates brought to the surface sentiments of inclusion, exclusion, and his role in contributing to the school experiences of classmates who lived at the edge of his school world as an eleven-year-old. The story could be identified among "secret stories" (Clandinin & Connelly, 1996) that lurk just beneath the surface of a model professional self. As I read Shaun's writing about the power of this memory and Vicki and Janice's responses as they drew upon stories of their own experiences in relation to the one Shaun had shared, there was no doubt in my mind that the telling and the retelling of the stories could contribute significantly to shaping their sense of professional identity as teachers and teacher educators.

The existing professional relationships among the three co-authors provided a foundation of trust to write about times when they did not feel strong in their interactions with peers, but I believe that it was their willingness to be vulnerable that revealed the extent to which the stories they shared also opened up possibilities for engaging colleagues, and their audience of readers, in reflection and discussion about the power of previous experiences in contributing to a sense of professional identity. By opening themselves up to explore the stories among themselves, and documenting the sharing of details, they invite the reader to engage in their own processes of examining and learning about the potential of long-ago stories in contributing to a sense of professional identity in their current work.

As I read, I was also struck by the potential for differences in perspective as Shaun wrote that the event described that had lingered in his mind from decades earlier and that has been so powerful in shaping his professional identity was not remembered by his father who was present and witnessed the same event. This realization highlights the extent of differences in perspective in contributing to and shaping our knowing or understanding of events; not only did Shaun's father not see the incident in the same way as Shaun had remembered it, but he had not even remembered it as a significant memory. How could it be that an event so powerful to one person not even be remembered by someone else who had also been there? Would a more detailed description have helped to jog his father's memory of that winter morning? Why is it even important that his father did not remember this event?

The difference in perspective that is evident from this example reinforces in my mind the importance of reminding ourselves, as teachers, teacher educators, and researchers, of the potential for differences in how we may see an event in comparison to how our students may interpret an event or incident. In some ways, thoughts about Shaun's story reminded me of Mary Lynn's pondering about whether she had offended her students with something she had said to the extent that they no longer heard what she had to offer even if it might be of relevance to them. She had likely raised points with her students out of her belief in their importance in contributing to her students' learning positively, but her students – looking at the landscape from a different perspective – may have interpreted her contributions as something other than helpful suggestions. Realization of these differences in perspective raised in this writing reinforced to me the importance of including in our teacher education classes opportunities for students to draw upon their own experiences as starting points for identifying, and then building upon, their experiences as a means of professional development to inform their understanding of their work with future students.

Reading Mary Lynn's writing as she pondered challenges of engaging her students, thoughtfully, in important issues in teaching when they may be standing on different places on the landscape highlights again the role of vulnerability, this time from the perspective of a teacher who is also a researcher. While potentially uncomfortable, reflecting upon such incidents is a way of acknowledging difficulties associated with teaching while also opening up the conversation to engage others in discussion about possibilities. Mary Lynn's description of a teaching interaction, along with Shaun,

Vicki, and Janice's stories all highlight the value of writing and sharing narratives as a means of identifying, and exploring the impact, and power, of stories of vulnerability as resources for professional development and learning.

Dixie:
Elaine has eloquently spotlighted the visible interpretive acts involved in this chapter, even braiding her own interpretations into Shaun, Janice, and Vicki's interwoven streams. Additionally, she braided interpretations of Mary Lynn's thoughts from Chapter One into this analysis, finally identifying vulnerability as a key player to our identities and to our growth as reflective educators. Through many conversations with Elaine and Vicki over the past year, I know that through living in the three-dimensional inquiry space of putting this book together, and through working, dialoguing, and writing about the commonplaces, our greatest discovery has been identifying the different, yet consistent way that vulnerability has emerged in each of the chapters.

Each of us felt great vulnerability through what we chose to retell in our chapters, and we noted the vulnerability of the other authors through the various perspectives noted in their retellings. Several important questions have emerged for me, which I hope others will inquire into because of the work in this volume.

- What caused each of us to feel comfortable enough to open this space of vulnerability? We did not *have* to excavate the "secret stories" or stories of tension. Why did we choose to?
- Vulnerability is, indeed, uncomfortable. Could it even be dangerous if made visible within grand narratives (returning to the Keyes and Craig chapter)? Do we live in vulnerable spaces when retelling stories such as those found in this volume, only in relation with others who may embrace similar vulnerability and reflective attitudes? How does a teacher educator/researcher choose to burrow *within* safe interpretive spaces, then broaden *outside* these circles in order to effect change or to impact others through narratives and narrative inquiry?

I think the inquiry into such questions is a valuable one given that the "possibilities," as Elaine stated, have been identified within the chapters in this volume. I know one of the many things I have learned from Cheryl – and I have heard and watched her say this many times – that what we do as teacher educators is all about hope. We cannot despair given the current top-down, competitive environment of our nation's educational institutions.

We must always hope, and through our narratives (and those of students and teachers in classrooms), we find such hope.

Vicki:
And, I believe, hope is the profound and powerful conclusion to the chapters of this book. Hope because it is the element that sets narrative inquiry apart from other research methodologies. The process of storying/restorying – construction/reconstruction of experience – creating and recreating identity – is the power of narrative inquiry. Narrative inquiry may be profoundly transformational at a personal level. Each chapter alludes to this epistemological and ontological challenge; the authors demonstrate the strength and courage to learn and grow through experience. Narrative inquiry opens possibilities within a broader, interconnected level as well. Individuals shape their world. In becoming wiser, stronger, and better individuals, we make our world a society we value. This process, I am reminded, is envisioned in the braided rivers. It is captured in the interspersing of the waters, the moving in and out – the birds that move betwixt and among – the environment rich enough to nurture the lives growing within it.

REFERENCE

Clandinin D. J., & Connelly, F. M. (1996). Teachers' professional knowledge landscapes: Teacher stories-stories of teachers-school stories-stories of school. *Educational Researcher*, 25(5), 2–14.

CHAPTER FOUR

EXPLORING CHRONOTOPIC SHIFTS BETWEEN KNOWN AND UNKNOWN IN OUR TEACHER EDUCATOR IDENTITY NARRATIVES

Mary Rice and Cathy Coulter

ABSTRACT

Purpose – *The purpose of this research was to make visible the process of analyzing our narratives of teacher identity.*

Design/methodology/approach – *These narratives of teacher identity were generated by isolating critical incidents and then drafting them as emblematic narratives. They were then shared with each other and compared against the tool of chronotopic motif developed by Bakhtin.*

Findings – *We found that our narratives, when filtered through the tool of chronotopic motif, reveal ambivalence about whether we desire to be known or unknown as teacher educators and as people. As we unpack our findings, we move through the tool of chronotopic motif, piece by piece, illuminating our stories by themselves, in relationship with each other, and against the professional literature on teacher educator identity and identity in general.*

Practical implications – *As teacher educators, we think it is important for others, particularly students, to be known. However, we are ambivalent about whether we want to be known and if so, by whom, and in what pockets of space and temporality.*

Social implications – *This research has implications for discussions of professional identity, role confusion in teacher education, and professional women in general. It adds to a growing body of literature suggesting that identity is a holistic process that factors heavily into what happens in the context of teacher education courses at a university.*

Originality/value – *Our chapter demonstrates to colleagues how to conduct a narrative analysis using a tool from literary theory.*

Keywords: Teacher educator identity; chronotopic motif; stories of identity

Dewey (1938) argued that life and education are organically entwined. For both of us, that is particularly the case. Mary teaches two to six credits per semester in her university's English as a Second Language (ESL) endorsement program. She also prepares new teacher educators to teach the courses in this endorsement and participates in the program evaluation and revision process. At the same time, she is a full-time junior high teacher. She teaches the Direct English Language Development class for English learners in seventh through ninth grades, the reading support classes for struggling readers in eighth and ninth grades, general education English classes for eighth and ninth grades, and honors English classes for ninth grade during the school year. During the school day, she lives in spaces with at least five different administrative designations. On the days when she teaches at the university after school, she might move across six or seven distinct types of educational spaces.

Cathy is an associate professor with the usual obligations of research, teaching, and service. As a mother of three children whose ages span across ten years, her obligations range from publishing to homework support to curriculum development to chauffeuring kids to rehearsals. She finds the life of a working mother moves her across time-demanding spaces to the extent that it is difficult to find time and energy for reflection. Since the personal aspects of our lives and the social obligations within our positions as teacher educators are inseparable, it seems natural to embrace narrative inquiry. This research methodology takes interest in "lived experience—that is, in lives and how they are lived" (Clandinin & Connelly, 2000, p. xxii) for studying our stories of our identities as teacher educators. Carr's (1986) notion of *coherence* requires "telling and retelling the story of ourselves to ourselves and others, the story of what we are about and who we are" (p. 91). Our *story to live by* (Clandinin et al., 2006) embodies the emblematic narrative (Mischler, 1990) of identity in the narrative inquiry discipline. The purpose of this chapter is to explore our stories to live by that come from our larger cycle of teacher educator identity narratives. We do this by using the analytical frame of chronotopic motif, a tool borrowed from literature theory (Rice, 2011). The use of chronotopic motif in this research illuminated our stories to live by of teacher identity, as well as the professional literature on teacher educator identity. The report of this research attempts to capture the dialogue between story, chronotopic motif as a metaphor for the professional literature on teacher educator identity, and the larger contexts of our identities as teacher educators.

USING CHRONOTOPIC MOTIF AS A RESEARCH TOOL

Using narratives to represent teacher identity is situated in a long tradition spanning many disciplines where narrative is a way of knowing (Bruner, 1986; Gilligan, 1991; Greene, 1995; Polkinghorne, 1988; White, 1981). Alongside this tradition of using narrative in research are scholars who have used literary theory to interpret narrative (e.g., Mayes, 2006). Both Mary and Cathy had already used tools from the literary scholar Bakhtin (1981) in our academic work (Coulter, 2009; Rice, 2010). Mary has an undergraduate degree in English and learned of Bakhtin in her literary criticism coursework. Mary liked to use literature theory to interpret research narratives because there was something comfortable about doing so, since that was such a large piece of her initial academic training. In addition to certain coziness, Bakhtin also provided ways to merge interpretations of events in literature with interpretations of events as humans live alongside one another, particularly in regards to motif and symbolism. The idea that human interactions and storytelling processes in the everyday sense could embody meaning intrinsically opened up possibilities for conducting academic work. Cathy became acquainted with Bakhtin's writings while completing her doctoral work, during which she was particularly interested in the use of Bakhtin's concept of heteroglossia coupled with literary elements to problematize the voice of the researcher in literary works of narrative research (Coulter, 2003; Coulter & Smith, 2009).

Bakhtin (1981) defined a novel as a demarcation of a literary system that was recognizable. According to him, a novel could come from a larger story and be set apart or bound according to the desires of an author. In trying to harmonize the pieces of a literary system, Bakhtin suggested that time can be organized into chronotopes. His discussion of chronotopes asserts the existence of two different types. The first type describes historic generic types of literature. The second type is called chronotopic *motif*. It refers to specific tools and semiotic processes that govern the genres of the chronotopes. The motifs are described in Appendix A.1. Compton-Lily (2010) summarized Bakhtin's associated meanings for her case study in literacy. While considering the work in the field of identity, along with the work we had previously done using Bakhtin's literary theories, Mary identified chronotope as a tool with the potential to interface with the work in identity from various disciplines as expressions that would reveal meaning.

As we muddled circuitously through the research processes of collecting, analyzing, and interpreting our narratives, we realized the four commonplaces of narrative – temporality, place, social, and personal, and inward and outward (Clandinin, Pushor, & Murray-Orr, 2007) emerge as threads through the chronotopic motif tool. Temporality ties in as the possibilities chronotopic motif held to situate time in stories. Place is stitched in as a location that is archetypal as well as actual. The social and personal pieces form knots as broad lenses through which to filter experiences as McIntyre's (1981) multiple interlocking narratives. While using the motifs, the stories constantly weaved together the inward and outward, initiating reflective processes that simultaneously reminded us of the research on teacher identity and caused us to grope for connections between our own and each other's stories to live by (Clandinin & Connelly, 1999). However tidy and self-evident these connections eventually seemed to us as we talked over the phone and in person at academic conferences, we must admit that chronotopic motif seemed to grab our attention inexplicably.

REVIEWING RESEARCH LITERATURE ON TEACHER IDENTITY IN RELATIONSHIP TO IDENTITY GENERALLY

In addition to the tool of chronotopic motif, we knew we would have to locate teacher educator identity as an established line of research (Bullough,

2005; Pinnegar, 2005) in order to make assertions about interpreting teacher identity narratives. Our first realization about teacher educator identity was that it overlaps with teacher identity, a concept about which there has also been substantial work (e.g., Britzman, 1986; Olsen, 2008). The relationship between teacher educators' identity as teachers results in role confusion (Ducharme, 1993) for teacher educators as they enact their responsibilities. Teacher educator identity is fraught with tension (Cochran-Smith & Lytle, 2004) that has been expressed as narrative layers (Lunenberg & Hamilton, 2008). We understood these overlapping roles and the tension that emerges while trying to describe ourselves as one, the other, or both. We were also intrigued by the word "role" in Ducharme's work. To us, that term opened space for looking at our identities from the perspective of the arts – as a drama unfolding – and the acts that we participated in while playing these roles as narratives that could be interpreted with similar tools. We felt validated in our desire to use chronotopic motif.

The narrative work on identity has largely focused on teachers and not teacher educators. Clandinin et al. (2006), for instance, assert that "teachers' stories to live by" or "teachers' stories which represent teacher identity" (p. 7) contain knowledge about identity that can be unpacked to yield understandings. Accordingly, teacher educators should also have stories that represent their identities and form stories to live by (Clandinin & Connelly, 1999). As we considered the notion of stories to live by, we thought not only about what stories we tell often to others about being teachers, but also about which stories run through our minds as we plan courses, make decisions about which projects to pursue, and decide how to make use of our days.

Narrative scholars are not alone in their work in identity. Lee and Anderson (2009) proposed that identity could be conceptualized as *essential* (built from within) or *ascribed* (imposed by others). Erikson (1956) is credited with the essential identity perspective. The notion of an essential identity also corroborates with the Aristotelian notion of *telos* (1998) or destiny. The *telos* of an acorn, to use Aristotle's (1998) example, is to become a tree. The ascribed model shares borders with part of Harré and van Langenhove's (1998) positioning theory where one either self-positions or is positioned by others. Gee (2001) also offered four ways to categorize identity, which are through an individual's inherent *Nature*, their relations to *Institutions*, the *Discourses* or communities of practice to which they belong, and the *Affinities* they have for which they may not yet be members of Discourse. All of these conceptions of identity build on or borrow from theoretical bases from fields like philosophy and psychology, and they also grow out of work in linguistics. Harré and van Langenhove's (1998) positioning theory has roots in speech act theory based on the work of Searle (1970) and others. In sociolinguistics, Goffman (1959, 1986) argued that people take up and put down roles using language as part of displaying and reinforcing identity. Grice (1957) proposed that several maxims exist for human communication based on the exchange of information. Tannen (1986) asserts that relationship building is a major purpose for communicating with others and that purpose affects the telling, not merely information exchange. The links between these various fields validate the use of cross-disciplinary tools for narrative analysis, especially when layers of communication are embedded in the story. The myriad perspectives about identity caused us to consider how we might ever unearth stories that would capture our own identities in concrete yet flexible ways. Often we found ourselves telling stories to each other, in almost apologetic tones, asserting something like "Well here is this story that I have, but I don't know if it is good enough," only to have the other person explain to us all the reasons why that story added a layer of richness to our work. Not only were we having conversations about our stories, but we were also uncovering the ways in which the stories we shared revealed perspectives from our identity research.

METHODS FOR INTEGRATING CHRONOTOPE WITH RESEARCH PERSPECTIVES IN IDENTITY

As we conducted an analysis that merged pieces of identity theory, chronotopic motif, the four commonplaces, and our own stories, we each developed rhythms of reflecting, writing, sharing, reflecting, and rewriting. Mary's pattern started with personal stories that expanded alongside professional literature on teacher educator identity. After reading about identity and locating a literary tool, she began to compose the report of this research. While applying the literary tool of chronotopic motif, additional ways of considering the professional literature in teacher educator identity and identity research in general came into view through Cathy's reading of Mary's report and as Cathy conducted her own analysis by drafting and crafting her own stories (Appendices A.2 and A.3). As we read about identity, read each other's stories, and wrote our stories and interpretations, our thinking turned back to the personal; we came back to the stories to see if the layers of meaning that had folded around them resonated with each other. In this process of restorying, she recalled another narrative that she had written several years ago and decided that it would complete the cycle of stories for this chapter when it was added to her initial story and the two reflective fragments that Cathy had been writing. Mary showed Cathy her second story and Cathy agreed that it should be used because she remembered that she had a similar story. She also asked questions that led Mary to think about how her stories interfaced with those already reserved for this project, especially the ones that Cathy had written.

The processes described above of sharing stories, asking questions, using professional literature, sharing more stories, and asking further questions reflect the use of broadening, burrowing, and restorying (Clandinin & Connelly, 1990) as analytic tools. We broadened our view to include the entire context of the story of teacher educator identity. Then, we burrowed into individual stories of teacher educator identity. We then had to restory this experience by considering what changes or revisions in relationships between the stories and between elements within the story emerged. The chronotopic motifs generated dialogue throughout this process by providing conceptual bridges between the broadening, burrowing, and restorying processes. The implications that using this tool held for our own identities as teacher educators, as well as its potential impact on the interpretation of the identities of fellow teacher educators, form the final sections of this chapter.

EXPLORING MARY'S TEACHER IDENTITY STORIES

Mary wrote this first story about an experience that she had in her university's bookstore in order to participate in research with a narrative collaborative group. The story started out as a sentence in a long list of sentences that she believed might emerge as *emblematic narratives* (Mischler, 1990) for a multi-university project where an entire group had decided to make visible the analyses of narratives of teacher identity.

> I was standing in line at the university bookstore waiting for someone at customer service help me find two books for my research that I had ordered, and for which I had pre-paid. The bookstore did not have these titles in their regular stock, so I had ordered them two weeks ago. I had been told it would take a week for them to arrive and I would be notified, but I had not heard back. I just finished working with the practicum students who had been assigned to me in a summer school program for migrant students before going to see if the books had come. I waited in the customer service line for 15 minutes, only to be told that I should just go straight to the regular checkout line. There, I waited for another 10 minutes. When I arrived at the front of that line, I told the cashier what I had come for and showed her my receipt and she went to look for my books. When she

came back with two books, I explained that I had only ordered one of them. I took the book that was mine, thanked the cashier, and started to walk away. As I was going, the clerk stopped me and asked for payment. I explained that I had already paid for the book, which is how I had a receipt to show her, and which had made it possible for her to go and look for my book. The clerk was hesitant to believe that the receipt proved that I paid, so she went to ask a supervisor. By this point, I was borderline homicidal. I was unsure as to whether I had the emotional strength to keep from completely losing my temper. When the clerk returned and cleared my receipt as proof of payment, I grabbed the book from the counter again and started for the stairs to leave.

When I looked up, I saw four teacher candidates whom I had taught on campus. They were standing in a group smiling and waiting to greet me. I approached them and asked about their student teaching and life in general. Then I went to teach my class in another part of campus. I was glad that I had not lost control of my temper. (Mary, reconstructed field notes, October 2010)

The second story Mary wrote after she had taught junior high for about two years. Mary had received e-mail asking for articles about policies for English learners in school. She did not intend to send a paper as a contribution, but she was motivated to write about her first day working with English learners in the school where she now teaches. This is the story that Mary wrote.

The day I started teaching English Language Learners was the day I learned that I could be invisible. Sitting quietly, I nervously played with the pen in my pocket and clung to my handbag. The maroon leather couch in the counseling office was the perfect vantage point for watching people walk in and out of the office that I had been directed to.

"Linda takes care of the ESL teachers," the kind secretary offered. "When she has a minute, we'll get you all set up."

Before she could make small talk, though, students began filing in for appointments with one of the two school counselors. The trickle of students built to full stream eventually becoming an inundation that ebbed only slightly when the morning bell rang.

Twenty minutes had gone by since I had spoken to anyone. No one even looked at me. When my boss, the principal, entered, the secretary tried to introduce me.

"This is Mary Rice," she explained. "She is going to work with the ESL students." The principal smiled, not knowing whom to look at exactly and then moved through the gauntlet towards his destination. He had not hired me anyway, the district Alternative Languages Specialist had. I continued to wait.

Eventually I did meet Linda, a gracious person, who, after some discussion with another counselor about whether I should start today, directed the secretary to take me to my classroom and my prospective students. We walked down the hall to the library and went to the back corner. Opening the door of the windowless former supply room, the secretary revealed textbooks from the 1960s shredded from student use in one corner, and a counter full of dried up tempura paint in various colors and shelves from an old refrigerator in the other. I could not believe that this was supposed to be a space of learning. There were five Hispanic students, four males, and one female, sitting haphazardly in broken desks in the center. The teacher I was replacing had her purse and was rushing toward the door, explaining how she had done me a favor coming in today. "Good luck," she offered, throwing her coat on. "You'll need it."

Not knowing what else to do, I sat down with the students and started to speak Spanish with them, asking them questions about their lives. When they addressed me, they called me teacher, rather than Mrs. Rice. They spent the remainder of the class telling me about themselves, their families, and their other classes. When the bell rang, the girl lingered to say how nice it had been to meet me. (Mary, reconstructed from text written in March 2005)

FINDING CHRONOTOPES IN MARY'S STORIES

Locating Bakhtin's (1981) chronotopic motifs in Mary's stories came through the iterative process of reflecting, writing, sharing, and rewriting described earlier in this paper. The following is a representation of the narrative layers of our story, the story of chronotopic motif, and the story of identity, particularly teacher educator identity in the research literature.

Road, Path, or Trail

Pathways in literature come in a variety of conditions, but often the most interesting ones are those that are in disrepair or have not been well trod. The idea of road or path does not show up directly in identity research. In teacher education, the paths refer to pathways to teaching or teacher educating, or through the tenure process. This pathway is uneven and fractured, according to Lunenberg and Hamilton (2008). These researchers' review of literature revealed that the stultifying nature of the pathway to and of teacher education results from the fact that some teacher educators were teachers for many years first; others never taught children or only did so for a year or two. Some teacher educators have doctoral degrees; others have a variety of lesser degrees. Some teacher educators engage in original research as part of the job responsibilities, while others are not required to do so. Consequently, teacher educators are often unsure what path they are on, and where that path is going. In Mary's story, she thought she was going to the bookstore to retrieve a couple of books, but what she didn't know was that she would reunite with former students.

In Mary's first story of going to the bookstore to get a book, there were several paths. One of these paths was the one through graduate school, which is why Mary had come to get the books. Another path was the one that led from the first part of her day, which she had spent in migrant summer school, to the second part of her day working at the university. Both of these paths, in their respective contexts, were well trod. The second story of going to teach English learners for the first time had a less well-defined path. The person who was leaving that job, so Mary could fill it was abandoning the path of teaching young English learners because it was murkier than the one she had experienced working with adults. The ill-equipped room Mary had been assigned to work in represented barbs and snags for her in trying to gather resources to help these students. Mary also realized that these students were not walking along the path that others were at that school. They took a side jaunt every day that was being sold to them and their parents as a short cut, or assistive in some way. From what Mary could see, it was not. Being in ESL class for three hours per day under those conditions was a much harder road if these children wanted to move forward.

What is intriguing about both of these pathways is that Mary's pathway and her students' in both stories are connected. Their paths are connected in each instance through shared space. In the first story, the shared space was the university and in the second, the shared space was that little windowless room with wide-eyed children sitting in broken desks.

Unexpected Encounters

In following a cycle of living, telling, retelling, and reliving (Clandinin & Connelly, 2000), we realize that even the time we perceive as being personal – no matter how much we tell ourselves that it is private – is not. Doyle (1986) argued that the main feature of teaching is its essential publicness. When Mary was new to teaching, she realized that publicness referred to the way in which her classroom actions would be known in the community. What she did not realize was that her private actions could also be made public with very little effort. In Mary's story of her experience at the bookstore, a teacher's actions are public because she is in public, and it does not seem that anything can be done to make that different. What was interesting to Mary as she conducted the analysis of this story was how, though she knows that this publicness pervades the path of her life as a teacher, she still finds it unexpected when some aspect of her teaching or her work as a teacher becomes public. Mary teaches on more than one landscape practically every day of the week. She should not be surprised that she sees so many students whenever she goes out and about. Perhaps her real shock is derived from the fact that these students want to interact with her.

Bullough (2005) explained that recognition of identity, whether it be ascribed or essential, is necessary for identity making. When Mary had a spontaneous reunion with this group of teacher candidates in her first story, it raised unexpected questions for her about the nature of her identity as a university-based teacher educator. She had to realize that her teacher educator identity was as tangible as her teacher identity. In her second story, Mary encountered students she did not know yet, and so the emphasis of her encounter focuses on the classroom space. This space was unexpected and therefore confounded her.

Crossing Thresholds

For both ascribed and essential perspectives, a core theory of self underlies many theories of identity (Gee, 2001; Harré & van Langenhove, 1998; Lee & Anderson, 2009). Goffman (1959) suggested that every time a person enters a new setting, they put on a different mask or take on a sociological role, but that a backstage exists where one can doff the metaphorical masks and reveal the true self. Knowledge of this role is what guides behavior in different settings. This blending of identity from within as well as without has made its way into teacher identity research. Bullough (2008), for example, speaks of possible selves, but he also assumes the stance of Aristotle's *telos* – a central underlying identity called a core self.

Mary's first story troubles theories of the *core self*, even when they allow for *multiple selves*. Mary and the employee at the bookstore were playing their respective parts of clerk and customer, but she did not know that she was also playing the role of teacher educator. According to Goffman's (1986) work, Mary should have been trying to maintain her temper so that she could maintain a positive image among her students, assuming that she had such an image in the first place. Since she did not know they were watching her, however, that is an impossible motive. Even when using just one theorist's ideas about identity, tension arises from the dual audience. In this story, the backstage to safely remove the mask disappeared because her books could not be located, and thus, her role as a university student was extended, and because her former students watched the interaction between her and the clerk while waiting to talk to her as a former teacher. To them she was not a fellow student at the university or a mere patron of the bookstore.

The threshold is the place of role experimentation where more than one identity can be held at once (Turner, 1967). In Mary's first story, she stands in two places, although she is unaware of it. In the second story, Mary starts out in the place of the counseling office and moves to the space of her new classroom. As she enters this space and the former teacher leaves, Mary was positioned as the teacher to those children in that moment even though she had only planned to come and meet them. In both stories, when Mary came into contact with students, she crossed a threshold where she became their teacher and accepted that positioning when much of the work on the relationships between students and teachers focuses on how teachers, acting as authority figures and models of learning, position students (e.g., Delpit, 1996).

Mystery or Magic

While it is difficult to gage the motivations of various students, Mary's reasons for spending time talking with them after leaving the bookstore counter may lie in research perspectives in teacher education. Pinnegar (2005) argued that one way for her to help her teacher candidates take up the practices she was promoting was to structure interaction, so her students would give her moral authority. To Pinnegar, moral authority is present when teacher candidates care about what a teacher educator thinks of them and their practice. It acts as a spell, under which teacher candidates engage in actions that would please the person to whom they have given moral authority. The granting of moral authority is part of the mystery, or magic, that sustains interactions between teachers and teacher candidates. This moral authority is just as spellbinding as the magical-ability students have to appear when you least expect to see them and the power they have to position you when they see you, even if you are not aware of their presence. Since these students were watching her as their instructor, it did not matter whether Mary saw them or not – she was still positioned as a teacher educator.

In the second story, Mary experienced what were to her, unexplained forces that allowed the students to live in such (what she perceived as) odious learning conditions. She also felt that everyone else in the school must certainly know about it, and since it was happening, they must not have a problem with it. In that moment, Mary was not just experiencing the English learners in the context of their school – she had been spirited back into her former adolescent world where adults act upon children knowingly and willingly. Although the context Mary had entered was probably more of what Nieto (2002) describes as institutional racism, not aimed at specific persons, Mary felt that the children were intentionally underserved. For Mary, the alternative was that the students must have some amazing powers with which they had successfully driven away one teacher already that year. Someone was deliberately doing something that caused these children to be cooped up in this tiny closet without access to resources Mary thought were necessary to learn. There is also magic derived from Mary's visibility. In both of Mary's stories, she is perfectly visible to the people she is going to teach, while she is less visible, or even invisible to others in the bookstore and the counseling office. And the students aren't visible to her until the moment of the role change.

Rogues, Fools, and Clowns

Teacher educator identity is a landscape of tension (Lunenberg & Hamilton, 2008). The fact that Appiah (1997) referred to identity work as *soul making* suggests the magnitude of effort required by a person to resolve tension and to reveal identity (Erikson, 1956). This tension plays out as teacher educators experience identity making as an exercise dealing with the lack of respect or prestige that other professionals and especially other academic are perceived to be enjoying.

The people who embody prohibitive positioning in the lives of teacher educators match Bakhtin's (1981) conception of rogues. In chronotopic terms, such feelings of not being listened to or respected describe fools. Goffman's (1959) explanation of the efforts involved in avoiding the appearance of foolishness in human interactions, while interesting from a sociolinguistic perspective, does not capture Bakhtin's (1981) conceptualization of the fool in a novel. Instead of a person who is unwise or unintelligent, Bakhtin's fools are described as people who are not valued in society, and yet say very wise things about society and about human nature. The character designation of a foolish teacher educator is not as unflattering as it sounds outside Bakhtin's theories. In both of Mary's stories, she asserts a belief that other people know things that she does not know and they reveal that knowledge to her through various signals. In Bakhtin's tradition, the person who realizes something that an authority does not and then communicates that realization is a fool. In the first story, the students watch Mary and remind her that she is a teacher educator. In the second story, the students recognize her as a teacher before she does. It was not until Mary engaged in the process of capturing and analyzing her own narratives that she was able to restory her students as Bakhtin's (1981) wise fools and herself as oblivious.

EXPLORING CATHY'S TEACHER EDUCATOR IDENTITY STORIES

Cathy also has two stories from her cycle about her teacher educator identity. Both of her stories were drafted in close proximity, unlike Mary's that were initially shaped years apart. The events and subsequent storying process had such an impact on Cathy that she was inclined to continue to story and restory around the same theme, though this only became clear to Cathy after she had constructed both narratives. It was only in the process of analysis in collaboration with Mary that the significance of both narratives in terms of Bakhtin's concept of chronotopes became clear. Cathy composed the following story after the second story she will tell. However, as the analysis proceeds, Cathy's logic in doing so is revealed.

> The four-passenger plane leaps off the tiny runway and edges over the Bering Sea before heading east from Scammon Bay toward Bethel. The outline of the coast reminds me of the small thin line of Alaska's west coast on a map. The engine noise makes talk impossible, so I look out the window at the expanse of flat, frozen tundra. The land is utterly still, though I know it is teeming with life. We are flying into the sunrise. It is hard to tell where the sun will first appear as, impossibly, we seem to be surrounded by the same pink edging all around us. It is a perfect morning. *The* perfect morning. We are suspended in time, watching as the sun embraces the earth. The Volcano Mountains pass underneath us. They are tiny replicas, the perfect form and shape, and I imagine that they, too, are suspended in time: Frozen mid-boil to revel in this morning with us. It is in this moment that the sun reaches over the horizon, spilling pink and orange across the snowy terrain. We are completely stopped as time flows by. The pilot looks back at me and smiles. A moment like this must be shared, if even with strangers.

Here is the second story that Cathy wrote.

> Officer Washington, the nametag says. I can't see his eyes in his reflective sunglasses. I would laugh at the cliché if it wasn't me that had been pulled over. Again. "Do you know why I stopped you, Ma'am?" he asks.
> "Um. No."
> "That was a four-way stop back there ..."
> "Oh, well, you know there was construction on the one side for weeks, and I just got in the habit of ..."
> He interrupts me, "You're in the habit of breaking the law, Ma'am?"
> I have the right to remain silent, I think. He rips the ticket off his pad and hands it to me. It says, "Failure to come to a complete stop."
> Again.

I stare at the words as Officer Washington pulls away. Not that it matters to him, but what I really want to tell him is that I've been up since four-thirty. Walking the dogs, packing lunches and backpacks, finding gym shoes, snow gear, homework. The home rush ends and the driving begins, icy roads across town to the progressive schools, art schools, anything that doesn't involve "the script." The work day flies by and I'm writing a lengthy to do list for home, packing articles to read, papers to respond to, readings. Back to driving, to rehearsals and snow boarding lessons, doing homework in the car. When we finally make it home between six-thirty and seven there's dinner, dishes, homework, preparation for the next day and a hope to be in bed by eleven.

And in the middle of it all, Officer Washington pulls me over and tickets me for failing to come to a complete stop.

The third time an officer stands at my window writing, me a ticket (leaving me just two points on my license) the ticket isn't for failure to stop. It is "failure to yield to oncoming traffic." I can assume the "oncoming traffic" which I failed to yield to was the white blazer that t-boned my car. The one I simply didn't see.

I have to wonder, if I can't see a white Blazer coming full speed in my direction, how can I foster reflective practice in my own teaching, much less in the practice of my preservice teachers? If I can't analyze a simple intersection, how can I analyze a set of data? Doesn't doing the work of reflection require pause? Time to think?

My ticket fines can attest to one thing: It is illegal not to come to a complete stop. In terms beyond traffic laws, coming to a complete stop is, at the very least, advisable. And for my work, it is necessary, at least sometimes, to stop. Ponder. Breath.

FINDING CHRONOTOPES IN CATHY'S STORIES

Cathy's stories are very different from Mary's stories, with each traversing different spaces as well as different periods in their lives. However, as with Mary's stories, Cathy's stories are representative of Bakhtin's (1981) chronotopes. An exploration of these representations follows.

Road, Path, or Trail

The spaces that Cathy navigates in her roles as tripartite professor and mother of three have her continually on the road. Though she lives a singular life, within that life she is at once researcher, instructor, community partner, colleague, and committee member who finds herself locating, driving, cooking, tutoring, assisting, scrubbing, domestic laundering, comforting, banking, doctoring, chaperoning, attending, applauding, scheduling, and accompanying, among many, many other things. From Goffman's (1959, 1986) perspective, Cathy is displaying and reinforcing identity as she participates in these various roles. Travel, it seems, is one of the bigger aspects of both of her roles, as she flies in and out of villages in rural Alaska and back and forth on icy winter roads in Anchorage.

The paths of Cathy's identities are often in conflict. These conflicts might arise in several forms. One form is time issues, such as when the Curriculum Committee meeting starts at 2 p.m. when she needs to pick up kids from school. Another form is conflicting roles, such as in being the instructor of teacher candidates who intern at her children's schools. A third form is represented in the stories highlighted here, on a larger scale by needing time to be involved in reflection, inquiry, and quiet thought while she is constantly on the go.

Unexpected Encounters

In Cathy's stories, the tensions that arise as she executes her various identities cause her to meet up with unexpected encounters. Cochran-Smith and Lytle (2004) remind us of the tensions present in teacher education, and such tensions are apparent in Cathy's stories. As she rushes from dropping off kids at school to meetings at work, she finds herself stopped in her tracks by Officer Washington. This is the second time she is pulled over for running a stop sign, having been pulled over for the same offense, in the same intersection, just a week before. Though Cathy finds that there are many unexpected encounters in her life that put her various identities into conflict, this is the first time that it occurs to her that her frenetic lifestyle has consequences beyond personal discomfort. The demeanor of Officer Washington makes this encounter unmistakable: Cathy needs to stop.

At the opposite spectrum is another unexpected encounter: the flight from Scammon Bay to Bethel. The small airplanes required to fly to and from bush villages allow no carry-on bags. The noise of the aircraft makes conversation difficult. It was so that Cathy found herself in the midst of a beautiful sunrise, with nothing to do but look out the window and ponder. The moment that the pilot turned, made eye contact with Cathy, and smiled was an unexpected encounter. Here was a moment in time when all obligations, both familial and work-related, had come to a complete stop, and the moment is acknowledged by the pilot, who through his glance and smile indicates that this is a special moment, one to be shared. What makes these two encounters even more unexpected is their polarity: Being pulled over by the officer was categorically unpleasant, and watching an amazing sunrise over the tundra was categorically pleasant. Yet, both encounters pointed to the same theme in outcome: coming to a complete stop.

Crossing Thresholds

The thresholds Cathy crosses during the course of her day are more hazardous to her well-being than she initially thinks. The stage on which her story takes place is not firm and stable but rickety and in danger of collapse. Cathy crosses a threshold when the unthinkable happens: She gets into a car accident. The back story to what the reader sees in the narrative is that Cathy was driving the kids home from a rehearsal in order to grab a quick dinner and change of clothes and get her daughter back for another audition. The tire of the car was losing air, and it was too cold for gas station air pumps to operate. More, she was sick. She had a sinus infection, a lung infection, and pink eye in both eyes. Wearing her new progressive lens glasses for the first time while driving in the dark, she learned too late about the effects on her vision. A threshold is crossed when Cathy doesn't come to a complete stop and collides with an oncoming car. The consequences of not coming to a complete stop that Officer Washington alluded to through his demeanor come to be, and Cathy can no longer ignore the fact that this lifestyle is not tenable.

A different type of threshold is crossed on the flight from Scammon Bay. Circumstances conspire to render Cathy unable to work on the flight. And then the morning is so bright and bold that Cathy is able to see the beauty in coming to a complete stop and living in the moment. In Cathy's stories, the chronotope motif of crossing thresholds happens through opposing means – the literal stop when Cathy's car collides with another and when Cathy is able to enjoy the sunset unfettered by work or family obligations. Cathy never knows when or if she is going to get the chance to have a moment to pause, which may make the ones she gets even more precious.

Mystery or Magic

The chronotope motif of mystery or magic is sprinkled generously throughout both of Cathy's stories. Officer Washington resonates with truth when he foreshadows Cathy's accident, operating within Grice's (1957) notion of information exchange. Further, magic happens when Cathy is stopped not once but twice in the same intersection, reinforcing the notion that she must learn to come to a complete stop before she causes an accident with potentially tragic implications, and further foreshadowing the accident that does, indeed, happen. Of course, this notion is both literal and metaphorical. When Cathy gets in an accident without serious injuries, which was miraculous, given the nature of the collision, it is because she failed to yield to oncoming traffic, or, one might say, failed to stop long enough to look carefully before she proceeded headlong into her frenetic life.

The flight from Scammon Bay to Bethel is pure magic, as the sun seems to rise, impossibly, on all sides. The feeling of being suspended in time is a magical moment, which is acknowledged when the pilot turns around and smiles at Cathy, at once communicating and establishing relationship (Tannen, 1986) as co-conspirator within the magical moment.

All of the elements of the two stories conspire to help Cathy come to the realization that she must change the way she is living her life. It is a magical conspiracy when the outcome is positive, and Cathy as narrator understands that something must change.

Rogues, Fools, and Clowns

Two obvious fools emerge in Cathy's stories, reflecting the final of Bakhtin's (1981) chronotope motifs. Officer Washington is a comic figure in his stereotypical behavior. Yet, he is also a wise fool as he portrays the consequences of not coming to a complete stop, creating foreshadowing for the car accident that occurs later in the story. The pilot is not a comic figure, but he is a wise fool in his acknowledgment of Cathy's awareness of the beauty of the moment. Both fools from the two stories propound the same theme of the importance of coming to a complete stop. Bullough's (2008) premise of the essential self is brought up against the notion that in order for Cathy's identity to remain intact, she must come to a complete stop, which is the central theme within Cathy's stories (Erikson, 1956). This juxtaposition engenders a sense of irony in Cathy's story.

A less obvious presence of this chronotope motif is Cathy herself, as narrator. Cathy is the clown, the one who allows herself to uncritically move along her storyline as though she has no agency, no choice. She is the clown who plays the victim of the circumstances in her life, which clearly reflects her social situation as a White, middle-class woman. As such, she hardly feels unable to story herself a victim. Paradoxically, she is also a clown when she fails to examine why she finds herself in the social roles of both mother and worker that seem to determine how she will spend her time.

DISCUSSING OUR STORIES TOGETHER

As we shared our stories together and supported one another through the analytical process (via telephone calls, e-mails, and writing together at conferences), we came back to Ducharme's (1993) ideas about role confusion in teacher education as well as Bullough's (2008) notions of recognition as an important aspect of identity in the context of positioning (Harré & van Langenhove, 1998). We wondered whether the role confusion we experienced was somehow related to the ways in which we positioned ourselves using the chronotopic motif pattern. As teacher educators, we think it is important for others, particularly students, to be known. However, we are ambivalent about whether we want to be known and if so, by whom, and in what pockets of space and temporality. One of the ways in which Mischler (1990) addressed the notion of situated identity in his work with artists was to suggest a polarization of identity against the forces individuals feel are defining their identities. As an example, he discussed how some of his artist participants narrated polarity against family members who were also artists themselves. Examples of these polarities discussed by Mischler included: successful/unsuccessful; using their artistic talent/not using their artistic talent; and able to cope with life's challenges/unable to cope with life's challenges. As we analyzed our narratives using chronotopic motif, the force that defined us was teaching and our dichotomy emerged as unknown and known. Our work became different from Mischler's in that we positioned ourselves in both parts of the binary, and we perceived that others also position us in this manner.

Appendix A.4 illustrates the positional possibilities for being known or unknown in a given chronotopic motif. The first option is for the teacher educator to self-position as unknown and then position those with whom she comes into contact to be unknown to her. The second option is for her to self-position as unknown and position others as known. The third option is for the teacher educator to position herself as known and while positioning others as unknown. Finally, the fourth option is where both the teacher educator positions herself and others as known. The same table can reflect the positioning where the others self-position and position the teacher educator. When we realized this, we began to wonder if maybe some of the tension we have experienced with members of other colleges or departments within our own college resulted from us failing to anticipate how we ought to position ourselves among them.

We also wondered about the consequences of the role confusion we see dominates our professional identities. Since we simultaneously live private and public lives, we try to put our best face forward in our collegial interactions. There is a master narrative about professional relationships and how these should look and greater expectations for how teacher educators should live both in and out of classrooms. Norms dictate that we should not reveal much about our personal lives in the professional landscape. Our stories of living frenetic lifestyles are uncomfortable stories to make public, particularly as they are current issues that we are still dealing with. What is at stake for us if others judge us for decisions that we have made, or for how we characterize our lives? Will we be seen as bad parents, bad professors, bad teachers, or bad people? We were also troubled by the notion that our stories, whether we are handling our lives well or not, are a part of a broader story of working women – that invisible narrative that women sometimes feel oppressed by.

Although this chapter has been a study in *chronos* – the passing of sequential, ordered time, we wondered about the boundaries of time for both Cathy and Mary when time was extended and thus became an opportunity for learning. In Greek rhetoric, this kind of time is referred to as *kairos*. We found that in the process of using the motifs to analyze our stories to be a moment of *kairos*, we were able to stop in the midst of the narratives we were living out long enough to come to understandings about them that would not have otherwise been visible to us. For Cathy, it was important to see the officer as a wise fool, as bringing magic to her story in that his role was ultimately one of caring, of keeping her safe. If she had not seen that, she would not have been able to move beyond the, "all this, and you want me to come to a complete stop?" part of the story. Cathy was able to see that she needed to stop and take the opportunity to take care of herself. In tangible ways, this has changed how she lived. She spends more time taking care of her health needs and trying to find other places of *kairos* to take the opportunity to enjoy her children, rather than trying to multitask to beat the ticking of *chronos*. For Mary, the *kairos* in her narratives occurred several places as well, one of which was when she was observing the bustle of the counseling office – engaged heavily in meeting the demands of *chronos* – while she was waiting to meet the English learners who would become her students. As Mary considered Cathy's stories of negotiating mothering and living an academic life, she wondered how often she would be able to notice the time passing around her, and not be a slave to it. This is particularly important to her as she begins with her infant daughter to engage in the same negotiation of mother/scholar that Cathy has been for many years now. Although there are trappings of transition in all of our narratives – transitions of space, time, responsibility, and landscape – our narratives hold together in those moments where, whether we liked it or not, time seemed to stop and opened a space for opportunity.

What do our particular stories about our particular lives mean for other teacher educators? We hope our stories open spaces for them to acknowledge and involve holistically – as we have done – as scholars. It also allows colleagues who read this and us to take up the tension of *chronus* and *kairos* to acknowledge and involve our own students holistically as they become teachers. We have a reason now to ask them to think about if they teach who they are; what they do to sustain themselves such that they can be fully present for their students; and how their identities as teachers, as men and women with cultural, religious, and sexual identities, with families, and so forth affect the decisions they make in the classrooms where they will live alongside children.

Analyzing our stories through these motifs helped us understand them more deeply. Analyzing them collaboratively and having the added task of making that analysis visible helped us make connections with them that are both burrowed and broad; restorying them helped us understand our own decisions within our own lives more deeply. In essence, we learned that sometimes, it is okay – even necessary – to simply stop.

REFERENCES

Appiah, K. A. (1997). *Experiments in ethics*. Cambridge, MA: Harvard University Press.
Aristotle. (1998). *Nichomachean ethics*. Mineola, NY: Dover Publications.
Bakhtin, M. M. (1981). The dialogic imagination: Four essays by M. M. Bakhtin. In M. Holquist (Ed.), *Forms of time and chronotope in the novel* (pp. 84–285). Austin, TX: University of Texas Press.
Britzman, D. P. (1986). Cultural myths in the making of a teacher: Biography and social structure in teacher education. *Harvard Educational Review*, 56, 442–446.
Bruner, J. (1986). *Actual minds, possible worlds*. Cambridge, MA: Harvard University Press.
Bullough, R. V. (2005). Being and becoming a mentor: School-based teacher educators and teacher educator identity. *Teaching and Teacher Education*, 20(6), 143–155.
Bullough, R. V. (2008). *Counternarratives: Stories of teacher education and becoming a teacher*. Albany, NY: SUNY Press.
Carr, D. (1986). *Time, narrative, and history*. Bloomington, IN: Indiana University Press.
Clandinin, D. J., & Connelly, F. M. (1990). Stories of experience and narrative inquiry. *Educational Researcher*, 19(5), 2–14.
Clandinin, D. J., & Connelly, F. M. (1999). *Shaping a professional identity: Stories of educational practice*. New York, NY: Teachers College Press.
Clandinin, D. J., & Connelly, F. M. (2000). *Narrative inquiry: Experience and story in qualitative research*. San Francisco, CA: Jossey-Bass.

Clandinin, D. J., Huber, J., Huber, M., Murphy, M. S., Murray-Orr, A., Pearce, M., & Steeves, P. (2006). *Composing diverse identities: Narrative inquiries into the interwoven lives of children and teachers*. London: Routledge.

Clandinin, D., Pushor, D., & Murray-Orr, A. (2007). Navigating sites for narrative inquiry. *Journal of Teacher Education, 58*, 21–35.

Cochran-Smith, M., & Lytle, S. L. (2004). Practitioner inquiry, knowledge, and university culture. In J. Loughran, M. L. Hamilton, V. LaBoskey & T. Russell (Eds.), *International handbook of research of self-study of teaching and teacher education practices* (pp. 601–649). Dordrecht, The Netherlands: Kluwer.

Compton-Lily, C. (2010). *Making sense of time as context: Theoretical affordances of chronotopes in a study of schooling and school success*. WCER Working Paper No. 2010-11. Retrieved from http://www.wcer.wisc.edu/publications/workingpapers/papers.php

Coulter, C. (2003). *Snow white, revolutions, the American dream and other fairy tales: Growing up immigrant in an American high school*. Doctoral dissertation. Arizona State University, Phoenix, AZ.

Coulter, C. (2009). Response to comments: Finding the narrative in narrative research. *Educational Researcher, 38*, 608–611.

Coulter, C., & Smith, M. L. (2009). The construction zone: Literary elements in narrative research. *Educational Researcher, 38*(8), 577–590.

Delpit, L. (1996). *Teaching other people's children*. New York, NY: New Press.

Dewey, J. (1938). *Experience and education*. New York, NY: Kappa Delta Pi Publications.

Doyle, W. (1986). Classroom organization and management. In M. C. Wittrock (Ed.), *Handbook of research on teaching* (3rd ed., pp. 392–431). New York, NY: MacMillan.

Ducharme, E. R. (1993). *The lives of teacher educators*. New York, NY: Teachers College Press.

Erikson, E. H. (1956). *Adolescence: Youth in crisis*. New York, NY: W.W. Norton.

Gee, J. P. (2001). Identity as an analytic lens for research in education. *Review of Research in Education, 25*, 99–125.

Gilligan, C. (1991). Women's psychological development: Implications for psychotherapy. In C. Gilligan, A. Rogers & D. Tolman (Eds.), *Women, girls, and psychotherapy: Reframing resistance* (pp. 5–32). Binghampton, NY: Harrington Park Press.

Goffman, E. (1959). *The presentation of self in everyday life*. New York, NY: Anchor.

Goffman, E. (1986). *Frame analysis*. York, PN: The Maple Press.

Greene, M. (1995). *Releasing the imagination: Essays on education, the arts, and social change*. San Francisco, CA: Jossey-Bass.

Grice, H. P. (1957). Meaning. *Philosophical Review, 66*, 377–388.

Harré, R., & van Langenhove, L. (1998). *Positioning theory: Moral contexts of international action*. Oxford, England: Wiley-Blackwell Publishing.

Lee, J. S., & Anderson, K. T. (2009). Negotiating linguistic and cultural identities: Theorizing and constructing opportunities and risks in education. *Review of Research in Education, 33*, 181–211.

Lunenberg, M., & Hamilton, M. L. (2008). Threading a golden chain: An attempt to find our identities as teacher educators. *Teacher Education Quarterly, 35*(1), 185–205.

Mayes, C. (2006). *The archetypal hero's journey in teaching and learning*. Madison, WI: Atwood.

McIntyre, A. (1981). *After virtue*. Notre Dame, IN: University of Notre Dame Press.

Mischler, E. (1990). Validation in inquiry-guided research: The role of exemplars in narrative research. *Harvard Educational Review, 60*, 415–442.

Nieto, S. (2002). *Language, culture, and teaching: Critical perspectives for a new century.* Mahwah, NJ: Lawrence Erlbaum Associates Publishers.

Olsen, B. (2008). How reasons for entry into the profession illuminate teacher identity development. *Teacher Education Quarterly, 35*(3), 23–40.

Pinnegar, S. (2005). Identity development, moral authority, and the teacher educator. In G. Hoban (Ed.), *The missing links in teacher education design: Developing a conceptual framework* (pp. 259–279). The Netherlands: Springer.

Polkinghorne, D. (1988). *Narrative knowing and the human sciences.* New York, NY: State University of New York Press.

Rice, M. (2010). *Narrating the literate identities of five ninth grade boys on the school landscape.* MA thesis. Brigham Young University, Provo, UT.

Rice, M. (2011). *Adolescent boys' literate identity.* Bingley, UK: Emerald Group.

Searle. (1970). *Speech acts: An essay in the philosophy of language.* Cambridge, England: Cambridge University Press.

Tannen, D. (1986). *That's not what I meant! How conversational style makes or breaks your relationships with others.* New York, NY: Ballantine Publishing Group.

Turner, V. (1967). Betwixt and between: The liminal period in rites de passage. In *The forest of symbols: Aspects of Ndembu ritual.* Ithaca, NY: Cornell University Press.

White, H. (1981). The value of narrativity in the representation of reality. In W. J. T. Mitchell (Ed.), *On narrative* (pp. 5–27). Chicago, IL: University of Chicago Press.

APPENDIX A.1: CHRONOTOPIC MOTIFS IN LITERATURE AND TEACHER EDUCATION

Motif	Associated Meaning in Literature	Examples of Associated Meanings in Teacher Education
Road, path, or trail	The journey of life; a general trajectory	Stories of negotiating tenure tracks as well as stories of coming into teacher education
Unexpected encounters	The idea of fate; points of departure	Stories of deciding to become a teacher and/or a teacher educator
Crossing thresholds	The concept of crisis, new experiences, or changing course	Stories of leaving teaching to become a teacher educator; stories of changing universities
Mystery or magic	The fear of unknown; a sense of not having control	Stories of preparing teacher candidates to work with theoretical children; stories of trying to understand the current school landscape
Rogues, fools, and clowns	The feeling of not being listened to; having ironic experiences	Stories of teacher candidates not enacting practices learned; stories of practicing teachers not reading or misreading literature

APPENDIX A.2: CHRONOTOPIC MOTIFS IN MARY'S TEACHER EDUCATOR IDENTITY STORIES

Motif	Associated Meanings in the Story of Being Recognized at the University Bookstore	Associated Meanings in the Story of Meeting her First Class of ESL Students
Road, path, or trail	Path through graduate school; path to the class she was teaching	Path to teaching; being led to the students by the secretary
Unexpected encounters	Not being able to get the book she wanted; seeing several former university students	Not knowing what to expect when she met the students; not expecting them to be in a classroom that was so ill-equipped
Crossing thresholds	Standing on the threshold of the new semester as both a teacher educator and a university student	Standing on the threshold of taking up teaching
Mystery or magic	Wondering why the students were waiting for her; wondering how it could be that they happened to be there when she was; consternation caused by being so visible; visible to the students	Wondering why the students were in such conditions and everyone else seemed to be okay with it; wondering what had caused their teacher to leave; consternation caused by being invisible, yet visible to the people I was going to teach
Rogues, fools, and clowns	The potential for her to lose her temper and become angry, thus making her look roguish, foolish, or entertaining	She has this sense that everyone knows things that she does not know

APPENDIX A.3: CHRONOTOPIC MOTIFS IN CATHY'S TEACHER EDUCATOR IDENTITY STORIES

Motif	Associated Meanings in the Story of Communicating with the Pilot	Associated Meanings in the Story of Getting a Ticket and into a Subsequent Accident
Road, path, or trail	A moment in flight (on the road) in which there was an absence of obligation from either role	Conflicting paths of identities as mother/university professor
Unexpected encounters	The moment with the pilot, who turns and smiles	Officer Washington stopping her in the midst of her conflicting roles
Crossing thresholds	Experiencing a moment of timelessness, of coming to a complete stop	Coming to the realization that in order to be healthy in whichever identity, she would need to come to a complete stop
Mystery or magic	The breathtaking sunset over the tundra, the moment of conspiracy with the pilot	The foreshadowing from the officer, the outcome of the accident that was serious but without physical harm
Rogues, fools, and clowns	The pilot, who acknowledged the moment of coming to a complete stop	The officer, who foreshadowed the wisdom of coming to a complete stop

APPENDIX A.4: POSITIONAL POSSIBILITIES BETWEEN TEACHER EDUCATORS AND OTHERS

		Others	
		Unknown	Known
Teacher educator	Unknown	Teacher educator unknown Others unknown	Teacher educator unknown Others known
	Known	Teacher educator known Others unknown	Teacher educator known Others known

CHAPTER FOUR BRAIDED RIVERS DIALOGUE

Exploring Chronotopic Shifts between Known and Unknown in our Teacher Educator Identity Narratives

Dixie:

Mary and Cathy use literary chronotopes as an analytical, meaning-making tool, with layered narratives presented as field texts. Because they have brought Bakhtin's work forward for this purpose, I was provoked to find additional connections in my personal readings/studies. I have been reading Maxine Greene's (1995) *Releasing the Imagination*; all of the chapters include resonances with literature and explanations of how Greene "taps" perspectives while reading to help her to "read [her] world differently" (p. 116). She advocates that we "find ways of being dialogical in relation to the texts we read together; reflecting, opening, to one another upon the texts of our lived lives" (p. 116). I felt additional synergy between this chapter and the Schlein/Chan chapter which opened spaces for thinking about cross-cultural interpretations and the silences that can be found in classrooms. Greene mentions in her book novels like *Cassandra* by Christa Wolf and Ralph Ellison's *Invisible Man*, reminding us of the *narrators* (which resonates with the *rogues/fools/clowns* chronotope) that present their stories as "the excluded that always recognize and understand each other" (p. 117). She elaborated:

> Ralph Ellison's narrator in *Invisible Man* speaks of the importance of bestowing recognition rather than invisibility on others; and I understand that I can only recognize a person like the narrator and others whom I meet against my own lived situation. I need to try to see at once through their eyes and my own—if these individuals are willing to engage in dialogue, if they are willing to offer clues. (p. 117)

I am attempting here to layer Greene's thoughts alongside what Mary and Cathy have so eloquently shared about the invisibility and hidden lives of second language students and Cathy's sense of invisibility and frustration, then adding to that Candace and Elaine's work (Chapter Five) inquiring into spaces where "cultural acceptance" may be found "throughout the curriculum." They, too, noticed silences among some of their research participants, and by layering their own stories of childhood and immigration with those of the Bay Street School students featured in their field texts, they have done what Greene advocated above – they saw through the eyes of others while at once seeing their own. The result of these narrative inquiries is that the ideas keep us from a "constrained existence." Greene (1995) shared that this "route" of being dialogical in relation to the texts of our experiences can "save us" and "keep us alive" (pp. 115–116).

As I thought over the recent months about the chronotopes in this chapter, I began to see the resonances between the chronotopic terminology and the terminology of concepts often used by narrative inquirers. Mary and Cathy found great resonance as the stories shared from their lives "called up" the chronotopes, "reflective of the shapes that lives take" (Connelly & Clandinin, 2006, p. 485). Bakhtin's road, path or trail" could represent the narrative "plotlines" in narrative inquiry, while the "unexpected encounters" could be compared to being "wakeful" or to the idea of "bumping into boundaries" as Clandinin & Connelly (2000) wrote. The idea of "crossing the threshold" is of particular interest to me; this term resonates with how narrative inquirers must position themselves in different ways through the processes of their research. This idea of the "crossing of thresholds" provides a useful metaphor to conceive of *which* thresholds we cross and *why*. The "mystery and magic" resonate with the uncomfortable murkiness and ambiguity in which narrative inquirers must live when we are not certain which paths (or narrative threads) will emerge. I recall my mentor Cheryl Craig sharing with me that she sometimes keeps file cabinets of yellow legal pads filled with field notes and transcriptions, and reviews them over and over – in the midst of collecting more – waiting for narrative threads to emerge.

Finally, the chronotope of "rogues, fools and clowns" allows us to value vulnerability in an honest, self-deprecating way. I was quite hesitant to share some of the tracings I did in the chapter Cheryl and I wrote. In fact, I continue to feel nervous with the vulnerability I still feel. Yet, by thinking of myself as a rogue, fool, or clown, I can smile and sense the innate friendliness in vulnerability – the willingness to let others see you with your guard down.

Vicki:
Yes, Dixie, I recognize your worry related to feelings of vulnerability. As I read the thoughts you included from Greene's (1995) writing, I wondered if vulnerability is not inherent in that process if we make meaning in the way she suggests. Vulnerability is necessary to the opening of our lived texts to others. Shaun talked about this in terms of his frail self. In order to enter into acts of interpretation, we lay our stories beside those of others, and in that opening of self, we become vulnerable. I see vulnerability, though, as the foundation for the process of the reconstruction of experience. And, that push toward creating a better self and a better world, is the real transformational power of narrative inquiry as a research methodology.

Related to the chronotopes that Mary and Cathy present in this chapter, I am excited by the rich example they provide for the implementation of this analytic tool in research. Overall, I am in awe of the many explorations of interpretive tools the authors in their chapters have demonstrated for those interested in using narrative inquiry methodology. I really appreciate the work you have done to draw forward the connections between these tools for thinking about experience. Once more I am pulled to the braided river metaphor. The interpretive tools we use are one more way that our thinking and writing weave in and among each other's streams of inquiry.

Elaine:
As I read and reflected upon Mary and Cathy's writing in this chapter, I realized the extent to which the multifaceted nature of the work of teachers portrayed in their work stood out for me. I found myself nodding as I read about how Mary felt that she was allowing different, and perhaps less desirable, aspects of her character to surface when she responded with frustration at the confusion of the clerk at the bookstore who did not seem to know the details of her delayed book order and payment plan, and understood her relief that she had restrained herself from responding in a more vocal, and decidedly less polite, way to the woman's perceived incompetence after she realized that her students were within earshot of her interaction with the clerk. I also nodded as I read about Cathy running from place to place, responsibility to responsibility through the course of an entire day as she moved from home to school to home to interact with family members, colleagues, and members of her community without pausing to

take a break, only to realize her exhaustion at the end of the day when she had finally had a chance to sit down. These responsibilities were included in the teaching and advising responsibilities that many are aware of as being important to the work of teaching, but what struck me about Cathy and Mary's descriptions of their daily work was the extent to which much of the responsibility involved work that teachers assume in the course of the day without realizing, or having others acknowledge it.

At the forefront of these interactions are the many responsibilities a teacher must juggle in the course of a day in interactions with students, colleagues, teachers, administrators, family members of students, members of the university community, members of the community at large, and random others whose lives are interwoven into the lives of teachers and teacher educators. These tasks and responsibilities fill days and consume the physical and spiritual energy of teachers yet they go unrecognized.

It sometimes surprises me that public opinion of the work of teachers is so much more simple and uncomplicated than that which is lived by teachers. Why is it that the nuances of teachers' professional work are so unfamiliar to those outside the profession? While more detailed and frequent portrayal of the nuances and complexities of teaching lives is needed in order to enhance public understanding and appreciation for the work of teachers, the added benefit of professional camaraderie when teachers have a space in which to share nuances such as those presented through Cathy and Mary's work should not be overlooked either. These professional and personal benefits might be considered rationale for the presentation and analysis of writing such as that shared in this chapter.

Cathy and Mary's writing about the tensions of moving from one aspect of teaching to another over the course of a short period of time reinforces the use of teacher stories of experiences to enhance awareness of the complexities of teaching. The writing in this chapter, as well as in the others, highlights the importance, and the value, of sharing stories as a resource for professional development. Examination of the nuances of the stories, through the chronotopes, also reveals ways in which teachers and teacher educators may feel the need to 'brace themselves' for possible criticism from those who may have different ideas about what should be done in teaching, and how challenges should be approached.

In the following chapter, Shaun, Vicki, and Janice present, and then examine in depth, powerful experiences of learning from their own childhood that have contributed to their current sense of professional identity as teachers and teacher educators. Related to the sense of some stories being more open to criticism than others, and thus, recognizing the potential vulnerability they might experience in sharing these stories, they also explore these sentiments in relation to ways they might contribute to a sense of teacher and teacher educator identity by exploring in further depth the intersections of teacher identity, tensions in learning and teaching, and stories of vulnerability.

REFERENCES

Clandinin, D. J., & Connelly, F. M. (2000). *Narrative inquiry: Experience and story in qualitative research.* San Francisco, CA: Jossey-Bass.

Connelly, F. M., & Clandinin, D. J. (2006). Narrative inquiry. In J. Green, G. Camilli & P. Elmore (Eds.), *Handbook of complementary methods in educational research* (pp. 477–489). Washington, DC: American Educational Research Association.

Greene, M. (1995). Releasing the imagination: Essays on education, the arts, and social change. San Francisco, CA: Jossey-Bass.

CHAPTER FIVE

CROSS-CULTURAL INTERPRETATION OF FIELD TEXTS

Candace Schlein and Elaine Chan

ABSTRACT

Purpose – *The purpose of this chapter is to explore and deliberate over ways in which culture may contribute to the interpretation of field texts while also intersecting the dimensions of time, space, and sociality in accordance with Clandinin and Connelly's (2000) notion of the three-dimensional narrative inquiry space.*

Approach – *This chapter highlights research interactions within a long-term, school-based narrative inquiry dealing with lived curriculum experiences.*

Findings – *The researchers gained insight into some of the nuances of interpreting field texts. In particular, this study highlighted the potential influence of the cultural, racial, religious, ethnic, or linguistic backgrounds of researchers and their participants in shaping the interpretation of field texts.*

Research implications – *The field texts that were presented and examined in this chapter shed light on key curricular experiences, spaces, and silences that might occur in relational and interpretive research stemming from cross-cultural experiences and vantages. This uncovered strand of inquiry interpretation has wide implications for qualitative work.*

Value – *Narrative inquirers and researchers employing other interpretive forms of qualitative investigations might be influenced to attend to the themes of culture in their work in novel ways. New understandings of researcher bias and the subsequent interpretation of results can be seen from a cross-cultural experiential paradigm.*

Keywords: Teacher educators; teacher identity; field texts; stories of experience

CROSS-CULTURAL INTERPRETATION OF FIELD TEXTS

In this chapter, we explore nuances of interpreting field texts while taking into consideration the potential influence of the cultural, racial, religious, ethnic, or linguistic backgrounds of the researchers and their participants in shaping interpretation of field texts. We present and examine field texts, and refer to Clandinin and Connelly's (2000) notion of the three-dimensional narrative inquiry space to explore and deliberate over ways in which culture may contribute to shaping interpretation of field texts while also intersecting dimensions of time, space, and sociality.

We highlight throughout this piece our layered understandings of our own and each other's experiences of culture and the curriculum via a series of field texts. Moving backward and forward in time, we discuss field texts that shed light on key curricular experiences, spaces, and silences. We reflect on the shaping of our stances as critical educators of "multicultural education in action" (Chan & Schlein, 2010; Schlein & Chan, 2010) in terms of personal, professional, and social exchanges. Moreover, we place milieu centrally within our interpretive work. We explore a cross-cultural envisioning of field text interpretation on the shifting landscapes of Mainland China, Hong Kong, Montreal, Ottawa, and Japan.

RESEARCH QUESTIONS AND OBJECTIVES

The research field texts discussed within this work stem from a larger project aimed at gaining insight into the experiences of curriculum among teachers, students, administrators, and community members within one school context. In particular, we engaged with members of the school community aiming to shed light on the following research questions:

(1) How do students experience the curriculum in a multicultural school and classroom?
(2) How do teachers shape the curriculum with learners from various cultural and language backgrounds?
(3) How do school administrators balance school programs and policies with the needs and expectations of the students and their family members in a diverse school setting?

While the overarching aim of the research project was to collect field texts related to these questions, the goal of this chapter is to illustrate how we made sense of our experiences on the research landscape. As such, the objectives of this work are: to explore our experiences with field text interpretation, to underscore our particular usage of the narrative inquiry analysis framework of the three-dimensional space, and to situate our shared and discrete personal and professional cross-cultural narratives within our field text interpretation.

THEORETICAL FRAMEWORK

This work presents the findings of a narrative inquiry, following the research tradition of Connelly and Clandinin (1991) and Clandinin and Connelly (2000). We make use of "stories of experience" (Connelly & Clandinin, 1990) as field texts for our exploration of field text interpretation. In particular, this work centers around the concept of the narrative inquiry field text analysis framework of the three-dimensional narrative inquiry space (Clandinin & Connelly, 2000). This framework reinforces the interconnections of data analysis across and between temporal, spatial, and relational elements of inquiries.

Our work builds pivotally on Dewey's (1938) connection between experience and education. Moreover, we attend to the particularities of school and classroom experiences of curriculum guided by Schwab's (1962) notion of the "desiderata" of teacher, learner, subject matter, and milieu. These practical sites for curriculum examination, or curricular "commonplaces" (Connelly & Clandinin, 1988), are useful for framing our pragmatic inquiry of curriculum.

We further consulted with literature in various areas as theoretical resources that informed our interactions as researchers in the midst of a landscape study. We employed Yonemura's (1982) concept of teacher conversations to explore our layered attempts at dialogical meaning-making as educators and educational researchers. Conle's (1996) notion of "resonance" was useful for shedding light on our interweaving narratives of research. We also focused on the notion of "relational narrative inquiry" (Clandinin et al., 2006) in uncovering our stories of narrative inquiry field text interpretation.

In addition, several strands of research aided us in contextualizing our field texts and the interpretations of our field texts. Work on cultural relevance (Banks & McGee Banks, 1995; Ladson-Billings, 1994, 1995, 2001; Page, 1998) and cultural sensitivity (Cummins, 1996, 2001; Igoa, 1995; Kouritzin, 1999; Wong-Fillmore, 1991a, 1991b) provided us with a background for making sense of our work in a multicultural school. Moreover, this chapter builds on the literature on cultural inclusion in schools (Chan, 2006; Chan & Ross, 2009; Nieto, 2000; Ross & Chan, 2008) and cross-cultural teaching and learning (Malewski & Phillion, 2009; Schlein, 2009).

METHODOLOGY

Over the course of one academic year, we situated ourselves in a seventh grade classroom at Bay Street School. We participated in class life with the students and their homeroom teacher, William, throughout lessons, recess and lunchtime yard duty, extracurricular activities, and class field trips. In consultation with William, we further engaged in tape-recorded interviews with the students in groups of three or four. We also conducted informal interviews with the students, William, other teachers, and the school principal and vice principal. We maintained extensive field notes after all of our interactions at the school. Furthermore, we compiled our own reflective field texts in response to our discussions with each other and our interactions at the research school site.

Upon completion of the field text collection phase of the study, we transcribed all taped interviews. We then analyzed our field notes, reflective field texts, and interview transcriptions to uncover central narrative threads among the various field texts with reference to the three-dimensional narrative inquiry space (Clandinin & Connelly, 2000) for field text analysis. We returned to the school to discuss interim research interpretations with William and to attend school events at William's invitation.

DATA ANALYSIS AND FINDINGS

Examining Field Notes Using the Framework of the Three-Dimensional Narrative Inquiry Space

We begin with a presentation of field texts written following participant observations at Bay Street School, where both Candace and Elaine were part of a long term, school-based research project directed by Michael Connelly and Jean Clandinin. These field text records represent a starting point for examining cross-cultural interpretation of the process of gathering and interpreting field texts from interaction with student and teacher participants at the school. For each of the stories we present, we examine the spatial, temporal, and social-personal dimensions outlined by Clandinin and Connelly (2000) as a framework for considering the influence of culture when analyzing nuances of interpreting and writing field texts.

Resonating Stories from within the Same Ethnic Group: Elaine Learning about Her Student Participant

In this subsection, we explore some of our stories of culture and research. Elaine begins with a journal entry, submitted by her student participant to her teacher, William, during the spring of her seventh grade year.

> An Interesting Time in My Childhood
> An interesting time in my childhood was when I was four years old, and my dad, my mom and I went to China to get my sister. My parents didn't bring my sister to Canada when they came, because their trip from China to Canada was dangerous. Because my sister lived with my aunt until she was six, she didn't really remember my mom. But when my sister came to Canada, she and I developed a very good relationship.

As Elaine read this journal entry and reflected upon the many possible interpretations of what the writing might mean for Lisa as a first generation Chinese Canadian, and about what we could learn about it as a resource for informing teacher education, Elaine needed to remind herself that any interpretations are, by nature, tentative. Understanding the field text included acknowledging that it was shaped by many factors that might not be initially apparent from reading the journal entry.

Through stories Lisa's father has told her about leaving China to escape the effects of Communism and having to leave her sister with her maternal aunt because the journey from China was potentially dangerous, Lisa knows that her family needed to leave under difficult circumstances. She has spoken about how her father speaks about Communism with scorn. She says that "he complains about the Communists all the time" and that if they (her extended family members) "get him talking about Communism, he gets really mad" (Field notes, October, 2001).

Elaine thought about how Lisa's journal entry revealed ways in which her family's stories of immigration may be connected to those of other members of the Chinese community in Canada. Reading the journal entry, and then talking with Lisa about how her father became angry when the topic of Communism in China was raised, highlighted similarities to stories she had heard from members of the Chinese community in Ottawa where she grew up, and in her family as aunts and uncles spoke of their own experiences of growing up in China and immigrating to Canada. A few were relatively uncomplicated stories of intact families leaving China or Hong Kong together and moving to Canada or the United States without leaving behind family members in China. More often, however, immigration involved separation of family members, and stories of secrecy and risk in order to move and settle in new countries. Elaine and her student research participant, Lisa, have in common stories of immigration passed down in their families through parents and grandparents who left China to escape the effects of Communism. Upon consideration of Lisa's story, Elaine brought forward one from her own history. The following is a story that Elaine has heard in her family many times while growing up.

Grandpa leaves China
My grandfather began his career as a teacher, and then later became a politician in the town in which they lived. My family comes from Guangdong in the southern part of China, so it was removed from the political activity of Beijing. Consequently, the effects of Communism did not reach their town until years later. Towards 1949, however, there were often members of the Communist Party who went into the town, looking for my grandfather and some of the other members of the Town Council. Since the community was a relatively small one and most people knew one another, my grandfather was usually informed by other town members when Communist Party members came looking for them. When this occurred, he went into the nearby mountainous areas with other members of the Council until the Communist Party members left. The last time this occurred, my grandfather watched Communist Party members go from house to house, knocking on doors looking for him. Realizing the danger he was in, he left for Hong Kong.

Prior to the spread of Communism, movement between China and Hong Kong was relatively free and my grandfather often traveled back and forth between the two areas for work. A month after his departure, the borders were closed, and he has not returned to China since. He sent money back to China for my mother, aunt, and grandmother but mail was often intercepted and they could not rely on receiving help. (Chan, 1999)

Elaine reflected upon how such family stories might reinforce her sense of connection to distant relatives in China. In much the same way that her sense of connection to distant relatives in China is shaped by the stories she has heard about her family's departure from China, she interpreted Lisa's sense of connection to China and her relatives in China as being shaped by the circumstances under which her family left China and the ties they maintain to those who continue to live there. Family stories contribute to shaping a sense of who we are in relation to our families and our ethnic communities. Through stories such as the ones Lisa has told Elaine about her family's arrival in Canada, Elaine learned about the role of political affiliation in shaping her parents' decision to immigrate. Elaine learned about the connection of Lisa's family to other Chinese families, including her own, through similarities in the circumstances under which we arrived in Canada. Lisa's family's story of immigration reminded Elaine of these stories, and highlighted similarities to stories she had heard in her own family.

As Elaine read the field texts and reflected upon what they might mean for teaching, learning, and teacher education, she thought about how the similarities in the stories that connect Lisa's family to her own might also reinforce a sense of belonging to other members of the Chinese community in Canada. While similarities build a sense of connection, differences in the context of childhood neighborhoods contribute to significant differences in experiences and how we may see ourselves in relation to others within and outside of their ethnic group. Through interaction with Lisa, her teachers, and her Chinese-Canadian peers at her school, Elaine became aware of the many ways in which her Chinese-Canadian student participants' school and neighborhood community differs from the ones she remembers experiencing as a child growing up in the 1970s and 1980s. Elaine's childhood experiences of balancing affiliation to both Chinese and non-Chinese communities highlight some of the complexities of ethnic identity development in a neighborhood where Chinese culture did not seem to be acknowledged positively in a public way (Chan, 2003). These experiences seem different from those lived by Lisa and her classmates in their culturally diverse school and neighborhood community. In turn, they contribute to shaping Elaine's sense of ethnic identity as a Chinese Canadian that differs from Lisa's sense of ethnic identity.

These differences carried over into both Elaine and Lisa's school experiences. Throughout elementary school, Elaine lived in a neighborhood where there were not many Chinese families, and where non-Chinese families did not seem to know much about Chinese culture. Elaine's family was one of two Chinese families in the neighborhood, and class pictures from elementary school attest to her and her siblings being more often than not the only Asian children in their classes.

Elaine's adult recollection of school experiences does not include learning about cultural diversity as a part of the curriculum. Instead, she learned about Chinese culture through interaction with her family, from Chinese literature and language taught in Chinese school, and through family stories. She does not remember Chinese culture, or any other culture for that matter, being acknowledged or addressed in school or in the curriculum.

Exposure to Chinese culture and language in the neighborhoods and communities of her childhood in Ottawa was stark compared to the support for the development and maintenance of Chinese language and opportunities for exposure to Chinese culture and traditions in Lisa's neighborhood and school community. Reflecting back on the lack of acknowledgment for Chinese background in school, Elaine thinks she began to view Canadian culture as the standard. Schooling seemed to reinforce the differences between home and school culture without validating the importance of knowing about home culture and maternal language. Elaine learned to keep the two cultures separate in order to fit in, but in doing so she also felt she was denying her Chinese culture in order to be accepted in the majority culture.

From a researcher perspective, reflection of these childhood experiences offer a glimpse of the lens through which the field texts written about Elaine's interactions with Lisa through the lens of a shared cultural heritage may have been interpreted. At the same time, it is also important to recognize the extent to which these interpretations are likely among many possibilities. In the next section, we move to examine nuances of factors contributing to and shaping ways in which the field notes were, and could be interpreted.

Relational Narrative Inquiry: Candace's Resonating Interpretations of Field Texts

Previously, Elaine highlighted ways in which her home experiences with culture and family stories of culture have served to shape her ongoing development as a researcher into issues of diversity in the curriculum. Candace explores here her experiences that resonate personally and professionally with Elaine's narratives. Making use of the notion of relational narrative inquiry (Clandinin et al., 2006), we also demonstrate in this section the multiple layers of interpretation stemming from our narratives, as we move backwards and forwards, inwards and outwards, and across contexts in delving into the research landscape.

Over the course of several years, Elaine shared with Candace some of her childhood experiences of growing up in a mid-sized Canadian city that was not highly culturally varied during her transitions from childhood to adulthood. Attending to these "stories of experience" (Connelly & Clandinin, 1988), we puzzled over the impact of subtractive cultural environments (Valenzuela, 2005) on ourselves as educators and as researchers in curriculum. As Elaine and Candace began to conduct research together at Bay Street School, we engaged in teacher–teacher conversations (Yonemura, 1982) with each other and with our participants, including William, the seventh grade homeroom teacher with whom we worked at the school, as a method of relational knowing in our research endeavors.

We had positioned ourselves in William's class in order to gain insight into the experiences of cultural diversity across curricular contexts. We were interested in investigating how students related to each other when classmates represented many varied cultural, ethnic, and linguistic backgrounds. We further desired to understand in more detail how teachers shape curricular experiences for diverse students, how educators connect with students from backgrounds different than their own, and how administrators attend to the kaleidoscopic voices of the school community in relation to broader educational policies and practices that align with the suggestions and expectations of the local school board.

Bay Street School offered us a fertile environment for the inquiry of culture and the curriculum on shifting cross-cultural landscapes. The school neighborhood is extremely diverse. In fact, the area is a historical stopping point for recent immigrants. Many of the surrounding organizations work with the school to provide a curriculum that incorporates the educational concerns of students from a wealth of backgrounds. As we look backward at this point in our research lives, we further find it helpful to understand our research efforts as the exploration of the negotiation of a "curriculum of lives" (Clandinin et al., 2006, p. 135).

Beginning with the dimension of place, we wondered about how students made sense of themselves and each other on such a diverse curriculum landscape. We also wondered about how a diverse classroom shapes students' understanding of cultural differences and contributes to their willingness to interact with students from different backgrounds. We analyzed our field texts from our time in the school and uncovered a story of multicultural education in action (Chan & Schlein, 2010; Schlein & Chan,

2010) that was puzzling for us. We noted that the homeroom teacher, William, was conscious of his role in the school lives of his students as a Caucasian, European male. He made great efforts to model cultural acceptance throughout the curriculum. Graded assignments included the presentation of family histories and the scripting of family recipes.

While William attempted to shape a shared multicultural narrative in the classroom, our field notes highlighted how the students had a different experience with diversity. Our field notes told a story about how the students interacted on in- and out-of-classroom spaces within discrete cultural, ethnic, or religious groups. This narrative thread in our field notes displayed how three of the students usually kept to themselves in the back of the classroom and corners of the schoolyard at recess. These students included one newcomer from Romania and two Canadian-born pupils of European origin. We wondered about why the three Caucasian students chose to isolate themselves from their peers. We further noted how one of these students, George, refused to acknowledge his own family background and history. He repeatedly told us that he had no culture and no interesting stories to share with us. We wondered about where he positioned himself on his school landscape and within his neighborhood.

George's unwillingness to articulate his own experiences with family culture also led us to question who we were as researchers in the school environment and how we impacted the students. Although we had been a steady feature in the classroom from the beginning of the academic year, George resisted our attempts to interact with him from his cultural vantage. We moved toward an interactional interpretation of our research efforts in gaining insight into the inquiry focus of culture and the curriculum. As such, we considered our interactions throughout the school.

The interactive dimension of social relations rose in significance throughout our field notes in acknowledging George's silences. We looked for other moments of silencing and other potential effects of our lives as researchers on the inquiry landscape. One day, a student from Mainland China, stated to Elaine that she hoped to become a teacher like Ms. Chan when she grows up. When Elaine told Candace this story, we discussed our position as potential role models for students. Elaine explained that she had never had a teacher from a Chinese background during her formal schooling. Candace then asked her if this was the reason that she had become a teacher. While Elaine stated that she had not thought about that connection between her chosen profession and her childhood schooling experiences, we moved back and forth in time to tease apart the meaning of who we were personally and professionally, and who we were within our study.

Space, time, and interactions continually guided us in our multiple and layered understandings of our various field texts. While we wondered about how the students in William's class understood their diverse lives as constructed together on a shifting cross-cultural landscape, we further attended to the shifting cross-cultural ground comprising our own educator experiences. Candace interpreted her interactions with the students from the standpoint of her own uneasy cultural identity. The following excerpt from her reflective journal explores her sense of a transitory, uncertain, and fragile identity.

> An Anglophone in Quebec
>
> I grew up as an Anglophone in an English–speaking pocket community in Montreal, Quebec; a city with a French–speaking majority population. I consider myself to be a proud Montrealer, Quebecer, and Canadian; however, this identity is sometimes challenged by those around me. For example, I remember a time when I was studying in college that one of my Francophone peers began a political debate with me. She asked me where I came from. I told her that I was born in Montreal. She said that since I was not French–Canadian, it was obvious that I was not a real Montrealer or a Quebecer. I told her that my mother had also been born in Montreal and that my father was born in Quebec, but that he had grown up in Ontario. Then, my friend said that she felt that all of the Anglophones in Quebec should leave the province and go back to the places from which they had come.

This field text taken from Candace's reflective journal illustrates how her own sense of belonging and cultural affiliation was placed within political tensions and challenged by others. Although she wanted to consider herself to be a native of Montreal and of Quebec, she was told by others that she could not hold that title based upon the language spoken in her family. Growing up, Candace also witnessed the political seeds that were planted with respect to the status of English speakers in a Canadian province that is populated by a majority of French speakers. With the adoption of Bill 101: The Charter of the French Language, Candace saw a division solidify in her hometown on linguistic and cultural grounds. Many of the English-speaking families fled the province; her family stayed. She learned to speak English in quiet, apologetic tones and to avoid political discussion.

When the students in William's class at Bay Street School hid their ability to speak multiple home languages, Candace strove to understand their experiences from the basis of her own upbringing. The students had opportunities to study their home languages at school, and the annual multicultural festival showcased the music, dance, and language traditions representative of many of the students' backgrounds. We explored this narrative thread of silence and/or cultural rejection in further detail from the perspective of our cross-cultural personal and professional encounters.

In exploring the field texts, we drew together many connections between ourselves as researchers and stories that positioned us in different ways on the research landscape. We further gained insight into how students and other community members might interact within a diverse school. Moreover, delving into the meaning of experiences of diversity for members of a school community highlighted for us the central contextualization of stories of experiences to intertwined temporal, interactional, and physical dimensions.

Moving forward, we continue to unravel our positioning as cross-cultural researchers of diversity. Both of us are teacher educators in the Midwest region of the United States. At the time of this writing, we are learning to acculturate to a new culture and to gain insight into novel dialogues of multicultural education in action (Chan & Schlein, 2010; Schlein & Chan, 2010) Our shifting landscapes force us to open our experiences and our research to new visions of diversity. In the process, we are learning to reimagine ways of being wakeful to the voices and silences both among our students as well as among our research participants.

There are many insights and challenges to interpreting field texts related to the behaviors and beliefs of individuals of different cultural backgrounds. In exploring the field texts, we drew together many connections between ourselves as researchers, and stories that positioned us in different ways on the research landscape. At the same time, we gained much insight into how students, teachers, administrators, researchers, and other community members might work together to establish multicultural education in action (Chan & Schlein, 2010; Schlein & Chan, 2010) within a diverse school.

Moreover, as we reflected upon our research relationships with our student and teacher participants, we realized the extent to which these relationships were highly nuanced. In addition to the importance of acknowledging the potential for sentiments of vulnerability of researchers and teacher educators as they presented and examined their stories of experience, issues of vulnerability also surfaced from the perspective of our research participants. Sentiments of vulnerability became apparent in various ways through the research journey, and cut across differences in position, language, age, and cultural understanding of ideas about research.

For example, we acknowledge that age and position might have impacted our work with our participants and shaped the research in different ways.

Both of us are adult researchers from the local university, and our preadolescent student participants were in seventh grade at the elementary school where we conducted the research study. Throughout the study, we discussed our inquiry process with their teachers and administrators, and we maintained ongoing communication with them about what we were discussing with the students. In our interactions with our student participants, we explained to them in age-appropriate language our desire to learn about their experiences of schooling and addressed their questions promptly and in ways that they would understand. At the same time, we were cognizant of age and position in relation to investigative consent, and we monitored this via assessing their levels of engagement with us and their willingness to share details of events that they experienced in the classroom, school, or community. We were careful not to push if we sensed the students did not want to talk about specific aspects of their schooling experiences or their experiences of interacting with peers and teachers whose cultural backgrounds differed from their own. In this way, we attended to the needs of our student participants and undertook appropriate precautions in our interactions with them such that differences in age, position, and role in the school were not unduly shaping what we learned from the students in obvious ways. Their enthusiasm to interact with us helped to confirm with us their willingness to take part in the study.

We also needed to keep in mind the potential for miscommunication when researchers and participants have different language histories. While issues of English language proficiency were not factors influencing our interactions with the students featured in this study, we were aware that language issues might be a factor in interaction with their parents. We consulted with the students' classroom teachers about how best to interact with the students' parents about this research project. We used consent forms that had been examined and approved by the university ethics review board and that had been approved by teachers and administrators in the school. We also kept in mind the importance of providing translations for families who might need them, and more importantly, the value of being available to the parents to respond to questions that might arise when we approached them with the desire to include their children's experiences in our study.

We came to see through the course of conducting the inquiry this attention to vulnerability in relation to age, position, language, and culture as a significant ethical strand in our work. As a result, we acknowledge here the importance of recognizing the potential vulnerability of student research participants and their parents, especially when the students are from cultural backgrounds different from those of the researcher. Consequently, we considered this ethical strand during our investigative interactions, and we examined this ethical component of our work during our field text interpretation and the creation of our research text.

To begin with, we kept in mind the issue of age of consent when interacting with the students. As students who are not yet adults, we approached the research process with them through consent from the students following explanation of the research project. We also sought consent from the students' parents for their participation. We recognized that this aspect of the consent process required much consideration, even when parents were provided explanations in their home languages, with translation when necessary. We recognized that there remains the possibility that ideas of research differ across cultural boundaries, and we were concerned that parents might not have understood fully what their child's participation in the research entailed, despite translations of consent materials from English to their home languages. Furthermore, as researchers who worked in the capacity of participant observers who assisted their children in their schoolwork, we knew that the students considered us teachers or teaching assistants in their classroom. From their parents' perspective, we might be considered teachers for their children, and as such, we needed to keep in mind that the perceived role we played in their children's learning might compel them to consent to their children's participation in the study. We realize this has the potential to be a factor in research involving students and teachers in general and was not specific to this study in particular but recognized the importance of being cognizant of the difference in position that might be perceived in terms of power as well.

The issues raised here might be considered "stories of vulnerability" that differ from those presented and examined in the Keyes and Craig chapter and Murphy, Ross, and Huber chapter of this book. Thus, we discuss them here as important factors to keep in mind when researchers and research participants approach research from different landscapes. These realizations surfaced in various ways on the research journey, and cut across variations in position, language, age, and cultural understanding of ideas about research. We became awake to the need for the consideration of stories of vulnerability even when researchers and participants represent members of the same ethnic or cultural group, as well as of the need to acknowledge the potential for miscommunication to be greater when differences in language, power, and cultural understandings of research are added to challenges of communicating about research. These factors highlighted for us potential nuances of conducting research with and communicating about research goals to student participants and their parents when participants and researchers represent different cultural groups.

DISCUSSION

Critical to our understanding of interpretation, whether of events and interactions with individuals of the same or different cultural groups, is the recognition of the importance of context. As well, we have gained an appreciation for ways in which details outlining the temporal, spatial, and sociocultural details specific to the context contribute to shaping interpretation of events and interactions. We are further mindful of the need to continually come to terms with new issues of identity that are situated in new contexts where the intersections of temporal, spatial, and sociocultural influences contribute to shaping situations in unique ways.

Furthermore, these layers of influences associated with research participants intersect with layers of influences introduced by ourselves as researchers into the building of research relationships with our participants, which in turn contribute to the presentation and interpretation of field texts. Layers of meaning portrayed in the field texts are considered along with layers of meaning introduced by the participants and the researchers, offering a glimpse of complexities associated with attempting to identify with certainty ways in which influences contribute to and shape interpretation. Our work as researchers in identifying and considering the impact of these influences necessarily involves a willingness to consider tenuous as well as seemingly well-connected influences. Moving from field text consideration to the consideration of research texts in this inquiry effort, we worried about the lack of structure/fluidity, and the shifting nature of our discussion/interpretation. Coming to terms with little certainty in the interpretation of field texts and the significant challenges associated with following threads moving across different dimensions also needs to be acknowledged, since specific sources shaping the nuances and intricacies of interpretation and analysis of field texts are difficult to extricate.

At the same time, possible interpretations may be explored as research participants and researchers work together to examine field texts. In the present piece, we offer a glimpse of nuances, complexities, and possibilities through presentation and demonstration of interpretation of field texts across two researchers. We consider our prior professional and personal experiences in shaping our relationships with our participants in their respective contexts. This examination of the process illustrates the extent to which field text interpretation may move across contexts, and reinforces the extent to which our relational narrative as two researchers work to offer additional and sometimes alternative perspectives, and an additional layer upon which interpretation may be understood.

REFERENCES

Banks, J. A., & McGee Banks, C. A. (1995). Multicultural education: Its effects on students' racial and gender role attitudes. In J. A. Banks & C. A. McGee Banks (Eds.), *Handbook of research on multicultural education* (pp. 617–627). Toronto: Prentice Hall.

Chan, E. (2003). OP-ED. Ethnic identity in transition: Chinese New Year through the years. *Journal of Curriculum Studies, 35*(4), 409–423.

Chan, E. (2006). Teacher experiences of culture in the curriculum. *Journal of Curriculum Studies, 38*(2), 161–176.

Chan, E., & Ross, V. (2009). Examining teachers' knowledge on a landscape of theory, practice, and policy. *Curriculum and Teaching Dialogue, 11*(1/2), 159–171.

Chan, & Schlein. (2010). Understanding social justice and equity through students' stories: Individual, familial, social, and cultural interpretations. *Journal of the International Society for Teacher Education, 14*(2), 35–42.

Clandinin, D. J., & Connelly, F. M. (2000). *Narrative inquiry: Experience and story in qualitative research.* San Francisco, CA: Jossey-Bass.

Clandinin, D. J., Huber, J., Huber, M., Murphy, M. S., Murray Orr, A., Pearce, M., & Steeves, P. (2006). *Composing diverse identities: Narrative inquiries into the interwoven lives of children and teachers.* New York, NY: Routledge.

Conle, C. (1996). Resonance in preservice teacher inquiry. *American Educational Research Journal, 33*, 297–325.

Connelly, F. M., & Clandinin, D. J. (1988). *Teachers as curriculum planners: Narratives of experience.* New York, NY: Teachers College Press.

Connelly, F. M., & Clandinin, D. J. (1990). Stories of experience and narrative inquiry. *Educational Researcher, 19*(5), 2–14.

Connelly, F. M., & Clandinin, D. J. (1991). Narrative inquiry: Storied experience. In E. Short (Ed.), *Forms of curriculum inquiry* (pp. 121–152). New York, NY: State University of New York Press.

Cummins, J. (1996). *Negotiating identities: Education for empowerment in a diverse society.* Ontario, CA: California Association for Bilingual Education.

Cummins, J. (2001). *Negotiating identities: Education for empowerment in a diverse society* (2nd ed.). Los Angeles, CA: California Association for Bilingual Education.

Dewey, J. (1938). *Experience and education.* New York, NY: Simon & Schuster.

Igoa, C. (1995). *The inner world of the immigrant child.* New York, NY: St. Martin's Press.

Kouritzin, S. G. (1999). *Face(t)s of first language loss.* Mahwah, NJ: Lawrence Erlbaum Associates.

Ladson-Billings, G. (1994). *The dream keepers: Successful teachers of African American children.* San Francisco, CA: Jossey-Bass.

Ladson-Billings, G. (1995). Multicultural teacher education: Research, practice, and policy. In J. A. Banks & C. A. McGee Banks (Eds.), *Handbook of research on multicultural education* (pp. 747–759). Toronto: Prentice Hall.

Ladson-Billings, G. (2001). *Crossing over to Canaan: The journey of new teachers in diverse classrooms.* San Francisco, CA: Jossey-Bass.

Malewski, E., & Phillion, J. (2009). Making room in the curriculum: The raced, classed, and gendered nature of preservice teachers' experiences abroad. *Journal of Curriculum Theorizing, 25*(3), 48–67.

Nieto, S. (2000). *Affirming diversity: The sociopolitical context of multicultural education* (3rd ed.). New York, NY: Longman.

Page, R. N. (1998). Moral aspects of curriculum: 'Making kids care' about school knowledge. *Journal of Curriculum Studies, 30*(1), 1–26.

Ross, V., & Chan, E. (2008). Multicultural education: Raj's story using a curricular conceptual lens of the particular. *Teaching and Teacher Education, 24*, 1705–1716.

Schlein, C. (2009). Exploring novice teachers' experiences with intercultural curriculum. *Journal of Curriculum Theorizing, 25*(33), 22–33.

Schlein, C., & Chan, E. (2010). Opportunities for Muslim education in a non-Muslim school. *Diaspora, Indigenous, and Minority Education: An International Journal, 4*, 253–267.

Schwab, J. J. (1962). The teaching of science as enquiry. In J. J. Schwab & P. Brandwein (Eds.), *The teaching of science.* Cambridge, MA: Harvard University Press.

Valenzuela, A. (Ed.). (2005). *Leaving children behind: How Texas-style accountability fails Latino youth.* Albany, NY: State University of New York Press.

Wong-Fillmore, L. (1991a). Language and cultural issues in the early education of language minority children. In S. L. Kagan (Ed.), *The care and education of America's young children: Obstacles and opportunities. The 90th yearbook of the national society for the study of education* (pp. 30–50). Chicago, IL: University of Chicago Press.

Wong-Fillmore, L. (1991b). When learning a second language means losing the first. *Early Childhood Research Quarterly* (6), 323–346.

Yonemura, M. V. (1982). Teacher conversations: A potential source of their own professional growth. *Curriculum Inquiry, 12*(3), 239–256.

CHAPTER FIVE BRAIDED RIVERS DIALOGUE

Cross-Cultural Interpretation of Field Texts

Vicki:
The tentative nature of knowing is the strength that Elaine and Candace bring to this work. They explore in very real ways the fluid nature of inquiry from narrative perspectives. I wonder if the tentativeness arises from the shifting nature of the identities of both the researchers and the participants, and perhaps the shifting contexts as well. I see, in this writing, that Elaine and Candace trace their identities through time and place. They place it in relation to the personal and social contexts of their living. This "thinking narratively" is evidenced in other chapters of this book. Here, I think specifically of Cheryl and Dixie's burrowing and broadening. Elaine and Candace extend these same fluid qualities to their shaping of their understanding of the participants. Lisa, the student participant featured in this chapter, and her teacher, William, are seen as individuals constructing identities within the three dimensions of narrative inquiry: making meaning of their experiences in relation to their histories, their contexts, and the interplay between those internal and external conditions over time. I see this awareness strongly playing through the Pinnegar/Hamilton chapter as well. Then, I perceive in Elaine and Candace's writing for this chapter an abiding appreciation and sense of how contexts are continually moving along a continuum. Social contexts change over time and the shaping forces leave historical tracings. I hear this powerfully in Schlein's reflective piece on politics in Quebec and in Chan's story of her grandfather. These are powerful illustrations of the interplays of narrative work that play such a meaningful role in the three-dimensional space. This theme echoes in the Murphy, Ross, and Huber chapter as well. The tentativeness nature of knowing originates, I strongly believe, in the belief that one's identity is never set; we are always reconstructing who we are and who we are becoming.

Dixie:
Vicki begins an important conversation about the processes and the wakefulness of time, place and sociality involved in narrative inquiry as demonstrated in this chapter. There are numerous benefits to beginning narrative inquirers, and to those studying the acts of narrative inquirers, from reading and analyzing the processes in this chapter. From the development of open-ended research questions, to the "how" of writing field texts and the "how" of bringing them forward for interpretation as they evolve into research texts, Elaine and Candace display their processes seamlessly in this chapter, culminating in discussion of the possibilities of their curriculum work centered in issues of culture. I love the way they describe their research experience "in a multi-vocal mode of investigation that leads to interpretations that are tentative and contextual, yet meaningful and resonant for curriculum stakeholders" (p. 18).

Of note, also, is their process of layering field texts (written from observations/interactions at the school) with field notes, reflective field texts, and transcription in order to find central narrative threads – then, "interim field text interpretations" with William. All in all, this is difficult and thoughtful work, housed in relationship.

Elaine:
As I reread this chapter and the responses to the writing, I thought about ways in which issues of researcher and participant vulnerability surfaced in different ways at different places in the research journey. Candace and I wrote about ways in which our own sense of ethnic and linguistic identity was fragile at certain times during our childhood as we interacted with those different from ourselves. We highlighted and explored ways in which these interactions may have contributed to our interpretation of interactions with our student and teacher participants on the Bay Street School landscape. Our prior experiences of diversity likely contributed to shaping our participation and interpretation of school life with our student participants in many nuanced ways.

As I reflect upon this experience of learning about and interpreting the stories told to us by our research participants in relation to writing presented by colleagues in other chapters, I was struck by other ways in which sentiments of vulnerability surfaced as well. Not only was vulnerability an issue for teacher educators featured in this book as they wrote about and shared their experiences of interaction with colleagues and students in their work settings, but issues of vulnerability also surfaced from the perspective of our research participants. I recognized the role of vulnerability in the process of building relationships with our student and teacher participants. Much like the interactions that might be part of the process of forming a friendship, the building of a participant-relationship involved risk in that we could not be certain how our participants might respond to our utterances and to our gestures to engage them in conversation about their experiences, nor could we be ensured of their willingness to share details of their experiences. Yet in the process of giving of ourselves and demonstrating our willingness to share ourselves through long-term commitment and participation in the school and classroom and demonstration of an interest in learning about the students' and the teachers' school lives, we built relationships from which we also learned about the nuances of their experiences. In hindsight, I realized the extent to which we needed to trust that with effort and time, we would be able to learn about the students and teachers' lives.

Dixie:
Difficult to accept and even more difficult to live with is the "tentative nature" of field texts – that it is susceptible to multiple interpretations. Elaine and Candace eloquently discussed and displayed this for us. They then moved on to puzzle over and tease the layers within the stories: "we moved back and forth in time to tease apart the meaning of who we were personally and professionally, and who we were within our study." I appreciated how Elaine brought herself alongside Lisa's story of culture and immigration, and hope that readers find this beneficial in providing ideas for interpreting field notes, given that the process offered Elaine and others opportunities to wonder over the interpretive spaces and associated ambiguity in order to cull the narrative threads forward. Notice how Elaine and Candace then worked within a shared analytical space. Candace's question to Elaine about the origins of her becoming a teacher opened a new puzzle for the researchers as to how the students considered them (as people participating in their classroom over an extended period of time). As they wondered about William, they also wondered about their own "shifting cross-cultural ground comprising our [their] own educator experiences." This relational quality to narrative inquiry research is a necessary piece that brings Elaine, Candace, and others in this volume the rare and meaningful reward of appreciation and insight – rewards they may miss if they did not attend to living alongside and involving themselves and their identities in the research.

Vicki:
As I consider the powerful chapter that Elaine and Candace authored, identifying aspects that are meaningful to me, I see ways in which their work

weaves into the writing and thinking of other narrative researchers. The theoretical frameworks we use along the riverbanks, tug us into different tributaries. Here, Elaine and Candace focus on immigrant experience and teacher knowledge, and they are caught up in the rivulets and eddies of that stream of thought. But, as they consider the narrative meaning-making process, the work converges again with other narrative thinkers caught up in another stream. Merging and mingling.

HEADWATERS AND TRIBUTARIES: MEANING-MAKING USING THE THREE-DIMENSIONAL NARRATIVE INQUIRY SPACE

Vicki Ross, Elaine Chan and Dixie Keyes

In the introductory chapter to this book, we invited the reader to join us along the banks of the braided rivers of narrative inquiry research. We hoped to convey through that metaphor the interconnections we find among the work of our contributing colleagues. As we conclude this book, we ask the reader to join us as we visit the headwaters and tributaries of this research tradition. Nearly three decades ago, Michael Connelly and Jean Clandinin embarked upon a study at Bay Street School (Clandinin, 1986; Clandinin & Connelly, 1992; Connelly & Clandinin, 1988; Connelly, Phillion, & He, 2003) to investigate teachers' personal practical knowledge (Connelly & Clandinin, 1985). Using narrative as both phenomenon and methodology (Connelly & Clandinin, 1988; Clandinin & Connelly, 1992, 2000; Clandinin, 2008) for this study, their work in the field was integral to the adoption of narrative inquiry as a research methodology in the, then, burgeoning study of teacher knowledge (Connelly & Clandinin, 1988, 1990, 1999), teacher education (Clandinin, 1991, 1992; Connelly & Clandinin, 2000), and curriculum studies (Clandinin & Connelly, 2002). In these areas, as well as in others (i.e., Nursing; Chan, 2008; Chan & Schwind, 2006; Lindsay, 2006a, 2006b), this research, which focused on experience, became well-established and expanded.

While we trace the headwaters of narrative inquiry to Connelly and Clandinin, they likely would recognize others that fed the headwaters of this tradition. Those others might include: Greene (1978, 1988), Eisner (1979/1982/1985, 1988, 1991), Fox (1985), Bruner (1985, 1990), Polkinghorne (1988), Schön (1983, 1987, 1991), Lakoff and Johnson (1980/2003), Miller (1990), Bateson (1989, 1994, 2010), Heilbrun (1988), Pinnegar (1995, 1996a,

1996b), Pinnegar and Daynes (2006), Hamilton and Pinnegar (2000), Bullough and Pinnegar (2001), Jackson (1990), Ben-Peretz (1990, 1995), and many others. This period was a rich and generative time in education research. While there are many who represent the multiple facets of narrative inquiry's beginnings, Connelly (2009) and Clandinin would also trace their headwaters to Schwab's (1954, 1969, 1971, 1973, 1983) influential role and, of course, the writings of John Dewey (1938). Where do we choose to begin the story? Given how connections trace back across lengthy timeframes and over complicated terrain, deciding where to start an account is an essential question to ponder in constructing a narrative research space. We would be remiss if we did not look at the braided river; there are many streams that are part of this river, including Barone (2001, 2011), Clandinin and Rosiek (2006), and Chang and Rosiek (2003).

From the headwaters of narrative inquiry has come a strong research tradition enriching several strands of inquiry in the education field. Significant contributions in understanding teacher knowledge, development and education have been made by Elbaz (1983), Elbaz-Luwisch (1997, 2002, 2006, 2010), Olson (1995), Olson and Craig (2001), Craig and Olson (2002), Conle (2006), Craig and Ross (2008), Latta and Kim (2009), Murphy (2011h), and Kitchen (2009a, 2009b). Excellent examples of how narrative inquiry detailed descriptions of the processes of school reform include Huber (1995), Craig (2001, 2003, 2006a, 2006b, 2009a, 2009b, 2010), Ross (2004), Kelly, Gray, Reid, and Craig (2010). While conceptions of curriculum infuse these works in teacher knowledge and school reform, others speak specifically to notions of curriculum in their work, notably Olson (2000) and Schlein (2007). Many use narrative inquiry within their work with preparing teacher candidates: Conle (1996), Olson (2008), Seaman (2008a, 2008b), Pedrana (2009), Ciuffetelli Parker (2010, 2011). Similarly, narrative inquirers describe the complexities related to applications of diversity and multicultural education. Elbaz-Luwisch and Pritzker (2002), Elbaz-Luwisch, Gudmundsdottir, and Moen (2002) and Huber, Murphy, and Clandinin (2003) write regarding diversity. He (2002a, 2002b, 2003), Phillion and He (2005), Phillion, He, and Connelly (2005), Chan (2006, 2007), Ross and Chan (2008), and Schlein (2009) explore issues related to multicultural education. Others use this research method to detail the intersections with students, teachers, and content areas: in literacy Murray Orr (2002), Keyes (2009, 2011a, 2011b), Rice (2011), and in math and science Ross (2003) and Sack (2008). Research using narrative inquiry to investigate the connections between families and children's education is making significant inroads to understanding schools and the lives and education of children – Chung and Clandinin (2009), Murphy (2011),

Pushor (2011), Huber, Murphy, and Clandinin (2011). Finally, in terms of studying narrative inquiry tools and contexts of study, several important advances that enrich the literature are made by Huber and Whelan (1995, 2001), Conle (1997, 1999, 2003), Conle, Louden, and Mildon (1998), Craig (1995a, 1995b, 2002), Craig and Huber (2006), Olson and Craig (2005, 2009a, 2009b), Murray Orr and Olson (2007), Huber and Clandinin (2002), Huber, Huber, and Clandinin (2004), and Huber, Clandinin, and Huber (2006).

In this book, many interpretive tools have been introduced, and illustrated. Murphy, Ross and Huber used layering as a means of thinking narratively, Keyes displayed tracing while Craig used the notion of burrowing and broadening, Rice and Coulter explored chronotopes in meaning-making, and Chan and Schlein utilized teacher conversations and resonance in their chapter. We sought to fill a need for beginning narrative researchers, but also those in the field looking for a new or different approach to moving from field texts to research texts. Ours was a fairly narrow aim.

We believe that Connelly and Clandinin (2006) would counsel that narrative inquiry is more than what we have brought the reader through this book. "To become a narrative inquirer means more than learning appropriate techniques of field text collection and subsequent interpretive process for the creation of research texts" (p. 481). We would encourage the reader to explore what it means to *think* narratively (Connelly & Clandinin, 2000, 2006). In the text, *Complementary Methods in Education Research*, Connelly and Clandinin (2006) share narrative inquiry as a "new methodology in education and in the social sciences," and explore "starting points" for thinking like a narrative inquirer and for using the commonplaces and the specific dimensions "in the spirit of checkpoints for a novice inquirer" (p. 479). Furthermore, their "considerations of designing a narrative inquiry" should be explored by those who are drawn toward narratives in research, yet fundamentally do not know how to begin. Our hope in following what Connelly and Clandinin have shared in the (2006) chapter is that narrative inquirers will recognize the longitudinal nature of narrative inquiry, the identity explorations involved, and the epistemological and ontological bumps and boundaries found in interpretation.

As we edited this book, we identified as an important goal the exploration of ways in which narrative inquirers might approach their interpretive work with field texts and writing. Additionally, we wanted to explore the notion of a narrative inquiry three-dimensional space in this text. Connelly and Clandinin (2006) speak of the dimensions as the commonplaces of narrative inquiry. "… (A)ll three commonplaces come into play" (p. 481). As commonplaces, these dimensions exist in relation to one another – none can be eliminated from the experience. They advise narrative researchers "to ask temporality, sociality, and place questions" (Connelly & Clandinin, 2006, p. 481). Each chapter in the book addresses the centrality of the three-dimensional narrative inquiry space in contributing to their interpretation of field texts. Each author asked questions related to place, temporality, and sociality, and focused their meaning-making on "personal conditions and, at the same time, with social conditions" (Connelly & Clandinin, 2006, p. 481). They unpacked place or a sequence of places. They focused on concrete, physical, and topological boundaries of place where the inquiries and events occurred (Connelly & Clandinin, 2006, p. 481). Each explored interpretive acts through the temporal dimension, the events, the persons, or the objects with "a past, a present, and a future" (Connelly & Clandinin, 2006, p. 481).

We close this chapter, and this book, with reflective writing that Shaun Murphy, Vicki Ross and Janice Huber contributed in response to the metaphor which centers this book.

Source: Photo by Bob Kelly.

They write:

Elaine's words, situated in landscape, speak to we three situated in our own places. As three authors, we are intertwined in our friendship, our collegiality, and finally by this process of writing. We have traveled together in our knowing of each other since our days as graduate students in different places yet connected through Michael and Jean. We have, all three, migrated to different places on the academic landscape and yet maintain our relationships with each other. Elaine's experience can be understood in relation to the words John Dewey (1938) wrote about experience, his ideas of continuity, situation, and interaction. The narrative commonplaces of place, sociality, and temporality – extensions of Dewey's ideas – also provide a way of thinking about those birds, their movement, their noisy calling to each other, the grasslands of Nebraska, and Elaine's visceral response to them.

> From our reading of the words, this word image emerged –
> (we) Stood in awe (with each other)
> Looking, listening
> (noting) the indelible connections between the waterways and the land
> Shallow, braided rivers (of experience)
> Weave, separate (calling us to attend to them)
> (the) distinctions between land and water ... of the braided river (are, just like the experiences of people) difficult to see
> (there is a sense of) vulnerability (in the face of space and experience, if you will)
> (through our) exploring, (thinking), sharing, responding
> (we connect, not wanting an ending, imagining otherwise)
> (the phenomenon that is described is quite noisy ... these are big, noisy birds by the thousands ... yet, Elaine's words fill us with quiet ... by standing in place, attentive we find peace and renewal)

Source: Photo by Bob Kelly.

REFERENCES

Barone, T. (2001). *Touching eternity*. New York, NY: Teachers College Press.
Barone, T. (2011). *Arts based research*. Thousand Oaks, CA: Sage.
Bateson, M. C. (1989). *Composing a life*. New York, NY: Grove Press.
Bateson, M. C. (1994). *Peripheral visions: Learning along the way*. New York, NY: HarperCollins.
Bateson, M. C. (2010). *Composing a further life: The age of active wisdom*. New York, NY: Vintage Books.
Ben-Peretz, M. (1990). *The teacher-curriculum encounter: Freeing teachers from the tyranny of texts*. In Curriculum Issues and Inquiries (Series). New York, NY: The State University of New York Press. A Hebrew edition published by MOFET in 1995.
Ben-Peretz, M. (1995). *Learning from experience: Memory and the teacher's account of teaching*. In Teacher Development (Series). New York, NY: The State University of New York Press.
Bruner, J. (1985). *Actual minds, possible worlds*. Cambridge: Harvard University Press.
Bruner, J. (1990). *Acts of meaning*. Cambridge: Harvard University Press.
Bullough, R. V., Jr., & Pinnegar, S. E. (2001). Guidelines for quality in autobiographical forms of self-study research. *Educational Researcher, 30*(3), 13–22.
Chan, E. (2006). Teacher experiences of culture in the curriculum. *Journal of Curriculum Studies, 38*(2), 161–176.
Chan, E. (2007). Student experiences of a culturally-sensitive curriculum: Ethnic identity development amid conflicting stories to live by. *Journal of Curriculum Studies, 39*(2), 177–194.
Chan, E. A. (2008). Evaluating narrative pedagogy in nursing education in Hong Kong. *Nursing Science Quarterly, 21*(3), 261–267.
Chan, E. A., & Schwind, J. (2006). Two nurse teachers reflect on acquiring their nursing identity. *Reflective Practice, 7*(3), 303–314.
Chang, P. J., & Rosiek, J. (2003). Anti-colonialist antinomies in a biology lesson: A sonata form case study of cultural conflict in a science classroom. *Curriculum Inquiry, 33*(3), 251–290.
Chung, S., & Clandinin, D. J. (2009). The interwoven stories of teachers, families and children in curriculum making. In M. Miller Marsh & T. Turner Vorbeck (Eds.), *(Mis)understanding families: Learning from real families in our schools* (pp. 179–195). New York, NY: Teachers College Press.
Ciuffetelli Parker, D. (2010). Writing and becoming [a teacher]: Teacher candidates' literacy narratives over four years. *Teaching and Teacher Education, 26*(6), 1249–1260.
Ciuffetelli Parker, D. (2011). Related literacy narrative: Letters as a narrative inquiry method in teacher education. In J. Kitchen, D. Parker & D. Pushor (Eds.), *Narrative inquiries into curriculum making in teacher education* (pp. 131–151). Bingley, UK: Emerald Group.
Clandinin, D. J. (1986). *Classroom practice: Teacher images in action*. Philadelphia, PA: The Falmer Press.
Clandinin, D. J. (1991). Learning to live new stories of practice: Restorying teacher education. *Phenomenology and Pedagogy, 9*, 70–77.
Clandinin, D. J. (1992). Narrative and story in teacher education. In T. Russell & H. Munby (Eds.), *Teachers and teaching: From classroom to reflection* (pp. 124–137). London: Falmer Press.

Clandinin, D. J. (Ed.). (2008). *Handbook of narrative inquiry: Mapping a methodology.* Thousand Oaks, CA: Sage.
Clandinin, D. J., & Connelly, F. M. (1992). Teacher as curriculum maker. In P. Jackson (Ed.), *Handbook of curriculum* (pp. 363–461). New York, NY: Macmillan.
Clandinin, D. J., & Connelly, F. M. (2000). *Narrative inquiry: Experience and story in qualitative research.* San Francisco, CA: Jossey-Bass.
Clandinin, D. J., & Rosiek, J. (2006). Mapping a landscape of narrative inquiry: Borderland spaces and tensions. In D. J. Clandinin (Ed.), *Handbook of narrative inquiry: Mapping a methodology* (pp. 35–80). Thousand Oaks, CA: Sage.
Conle, C. (1996). Resonance in pre-service teacher inquiry. *American Educational Research Association Journal, 33*(2), 297–325.
Conle, C. (1997). Images of change in narrative inquiry. *Teachers and Teaching: Theory and Practice, 3*(2), 205–219.
Conle, C. (1999). Struggling with time and place in life and research. *Curriculum Inquiry, 29*(1), 7–32.
Conle, C. (2003). Anatomy of narrative curricula. *Educational Researcher, 32*(3), 3–15.
Conle, C. (2006). *Teachers' stories, Teachers' lives.* New York, NY: Nova Science Publishers.
Conle, C., Louden, W., & Mildon, D. (1998). Tensions and intentions in group inquiry: A self-study. In M. L. Hamilton (Ed.), *Reconceptualizing teacher practice: Self-study in teacher education* (pp. 178–194). Bristol, PA: Falmer Press.
Connelly, F. M. (2009). Bridges from then to now and them to us: Narrative threads on the landscape of 'the practical'. In E. C. Short & L. J. Waks (Eds.), *Leaders in curriculum studies: Intellectual self-portraits* (pp. 39–54). Rotterdam: Sense Publishers.
Connelly, F. M., & Clandinin, D. J. (1985). Personal practical knowledge and the modes of knowing: Relevance for teaching and learning. In E. Eisner (Ed.), *Learning and teaching ways of knowing: The eighty-fourth yearbook of the National Society for the Study of Education* (pp. 174–198). Chicago, IL: University of Chicago Press.
Connelly, F. M., & Clandinin, D. J. (1988). *Teachers as curriculum planners: Narratives of experience.* New York, NY: Teachers College Press.
Connelly, F. M., & Clandinin, D. J. (1990). Stories of experience and narrative inquiry. *Educational Researcher, 19*(5), 2–14.
Connelly, F. M., & Clandinin, D. J. (Eds.). (1999). *Shaping a professional identity: Stories of educational practice.* New York, NY: Teachers College Press.
Connelly, F. M., & Clandinin, D. J. (2000). Teacher education – A question of teacher knowledge. In A. Scott & J. Freeman-Moir (Eds.), *Tomorrow's teachers: International and critical perspectives on teacher education* (pp. 89–105). Christ Church: Canterbury Press.
Connelly, F. M., & Clandinin, D. J. (2006). Narrative inquiry. In J. Green, G. Camilli & P. Elmore (Eds.), *Handbook of complementary methods in educational research* (pp. 477–489). Washington, DC: American Educational Research Association.
Connelly, F. M., Phillion, J., & He, M. (2003). An exploration of narrative inquiry into multiculturalism in education: Reflecting on two decades of research in an inner-city Canadian community school. *Curriculum Inquiry, 33*(4), 363–384.
Craig, C. (1995a). Dilemmas in crossing the boundaries on the professional knowledge landscape. In D. J. Clandinin & F. M. Connelly (Eds.), *Teachers' professional knowledge landscapes.* New York, NY: Teachers College Press.

Craig, C. (1995b). Knowledge communities: A way of making sense of how beginning teachers come to know. *Curriculum Inquiry*, *25*(2), 151–175.
Craig, C. (2001). The relationships between and among teacher knowledge, communities of knowing, and top down school reform: A case of "The Monkey's Paw. *Curriculum Inquiry*, *31*(3), 303–331.
Craig, C. (2002). The conduit: A meta-level analysis of lives lived and stories told. *Teachers and Teaching: Theory and Practice*, *8*(2), 197–221.
Craig, C. (2003). *Narrative inquiries of school reform: Storied lives, storied landscapes, storied metaphors*. Greenwich, CT: Information Age Publishing.
Craig, C. (2006a). Why is dissemination so difficult? The nature of teacher knowledge and the spread of school reform. *American Educational Research Journal*, *43*(2), 257–293.
Craig, C. (2006b). Change, changing, and being changed: A self-study of a teacher educator's becoming real in the throes of urban school reform. *Studying Teacher Education*, *2*(1), 105–116.
Craig, C. (2009a). Research in the midst of organized school reform: Versions of teacher community in tension. *American Educational Research Journal*, *46*(2), 598–619.
Craig, C. (2009b). The contested classroom space: A decade of lived education policy in Texas schools. *American Educational Research Journal*, *46*(4), 1034–1059.
Craig, C. (2010). Change, changing, and being changed: A study of self in the throes of multiple accountability demands. *Studying Teacher Education*, *6*(1), 63–73.
Craig, C., & Huber, J. (2006). Relational reverberations: Shaping and reshaping narrative inquiries in the midst of storied lives and contexts. In D. Jean Clandinin (Ed.), *Handbook of narrative inquiry* (pp. 251–279). Thousand Oaks, CA: Sage.
Craig, C., & Olson, M. (2002). The development of teachers' narrative authority in knowledge communities: A narrative approach to teacher learning. In N. Lyons & V. LaBoskey (Eds.), *Narrative inquiry in practice: Advancing the knowledge of teaching* (pp. 115–129). New York, NY: Teachers College Press.
Craig, C., & Ross, V. (2008). Cultivating teachers as curriculum makers. In F. M. Connelly (Ed.), *Sage handbook of curriculum and instruction* (pp. 282–305). Thousand Oaks, CA: Sage.
Dewey, J. (1938). *Experience and education*. New York, NY: Collier.
Eisner, E. W. (1982). *Cognition and curriculum: a basis for deciding what to teach*. New York, NY: Longman.
Eisner, E. W. (1985/1994). *The educational imagination: on the design and evaluation of school programs*. New York, NY: Macmillan.
Eisner, E. W. (1988). The primacy of experience and the politics of method. *Educational Researcher*, *17*(5), 15–20.
Eisner, E. W. (1991). *The enlightened eye: Qualitative inquiry and the enhancement of educational practice*. New York, NY: Macmillan.
Elbaz, F. (1983). *Teacher thinking: A study of practical knowledge*. London: Croon Helm.
Elbaz-Luwisch, F. (1997). Narrative research: Political issues and implications. *Teaching and Teacher Education*, *13*(1), 75–83.
Elbaz-Luwisch, F. (2002). Writing as inquiry: Storying the teaching self in writing workshops. *Curriculum Inquiry*, *32*(4), 403–428.
Elbaz-Luwisch, F. (2006). Studying teachers' lives and experiences: Narrative inquiry into K-12 teaching. In D. J. Clandinin (Ed.), *Handbook of narrative inquiry: Mapping a methodology* (pp. 357–382). Thousand Oaks, CA: Sage.

Elbaz-Luwisch, F. (2010). Narrative inquiry: Wakeful engagement with educational experience. *Curriculum Inquiry, 40*(2), 265–281.
Elbaz-Luwisch, F., Gudmundsdottir, S., & Moen, T. (2002). The multivoicedness of classrooms: Bakhtin and narratives of teaching. In H. Heikkinen, R. Huttenen & L. Syrjala (Eds.), *Biographical research and narrativity* (pp. 197–218). Jyväskylä: SoPhi Press.
Elbaz-Luwisch, F., & Pritzker, D. (2002). Writing workshops in teacher education: Making a space for feeling and diversity. *Asia Pacific Journal of Teacher Education, 30*(3), 277–289.
Fox, S. (1985). The vitality of theory in Schwab's conception of the practical. *Curriculum Inquiry, 15*(1), 63–87.
Greene, M. (1978). *Landscapes of learning*. New York, NY: Teacher's College Press.
Greene, M. (1988). *The dialectic of freedom*. New York, NY: Teacher's College Press.
Hamilton, M. L., & Pinnegar, S. (2000). Trustworthiness in teacher education. *Journal of Teacher Education, 51*(3), 234–240.
He, M. F. (2002a). A narrative inquiry of cross-cultural lives: Lives in Canada. *Journal of Curriculum Studies, 34*(3), 323–342.
He, M. F. (2002b). A narrative inquiry of cross-cultural lives: Lives in North American academy. *Journal of Curriculum Studies, 34*(5), 513–533.
He, M. F. (2003). *A river forever flowing: Cross-cultural lives and identities in the multicultural landscape*. Greenwich, CT: Information Age.
Heilbrun, C. (1988). *Writing a woman's life*. New York, NY: Ballantine Books.
Huber, J. (1995). Failed teacher professional development. In D. J. Clandinin & F. M. Connelly (Eds.), *Teachers' professional knowledge landscapes* (pp. 111–117). New York, NY: Teachers College Press.
Huber, J., & Clandinin, D. J. (2002). Ethical dilemmas in relational narrative inquiry with children. *Qualitative inquiry, 8*(6), 181–198.
Huber, J., Murphy, M. S., & Clandinin, D. J. (2003). Creating communities of cultural imagination: Negotiating a curriculum of diversity. *Curriculum Inquiry, 33*(4), 343–362.
Huber, J., Murphy, M. S., & Clandinin, D. J. (2011). *Places of curriculum making: Narrative inquiries into children's lives in motion*. Bingley, UK: Emerald Group.
Huber, J., & Whelan, K. (1995). Knowledge communities in the classroom. In D. J. Clandinin & F. M. Connelly (Eds.), *Teachers' professional knowledge landscapes* (pp. 142–150). New York, NY: Teachers College Press.
Huber, J., & Whelan, K. (2001). Beyond the still pond: Community as growing edges. *Reflective Practice, 2*(2), 221–236.
Huber, M., Clandinin, D. J., & Huber, J. (2006). Relational responsibilities of narrative inquiries. *Curriculum and Teaching Dialogue, 8*(1/2), 192–209.
Huber, M., Huber, J., & Clandinin, D. J. (2004). Moments of tension: Resistance as expressions of narrative coherence in stories to learn by. *Reflective Practice, 5*(2), 181–198.
Jackson, P. W. (1990). *Life in classrooms*. New York, NY: Holt, Rinehart & Winston.
Kelly, M., Gray, P., Reid, D., & Craig, C. (2010). Within K-12 schools for school reform: What does it take? In N. Lyons (Ed.), *Handbook of reflection and reflective practice: Mapping a way of knowing for professional reflective inquiry* (pp. 273–298). New York, NY: Springer-Verlag.
Keyes, D. (2009). Narratives of critical literacy: Critical consciousness and curriculum-making at the middle level. *Critical Literacy: Theories and Practices, 4*(2), 42–55.

Keyes, D. (2011a). Sunshine and shadows: Opening spaces for creativity, metaphor, and paradox in teaching and teacher education. In C. Craig & L. Deretechin (Eds.), *Cultivating curious and creative minds: The role of teachers and teacher educators* (Vol. 2). Lanham, MD: Rowman & Littlefield.

Keyes, D. (2011b). Making curriculum of lives: Living a story of critical literacy. In J. Kitchen, D. Parker & D. Pushor (Eds.), *Narrative inquiries into curriculum making in teacher education* (pp. 239–260). Bingley, UK: Emerald Group.

Kitchen, J. (2009a). Passages: Improving teacher education through narrative self-study. In L. Fitzgerald, M. Heston & D. Tidwell (Eds.), *Research methods for the self-study of practice* (pp. 35–51). The Netherlands: Springer.

Kitchen, J. (2009b). *Relational teacher development: A quest for meaning in the garden of teacher experience*. Cologne, Germany: Lambert Academic press.

Lakoff, G., & Johnson, M. (1980/2003). *Metaphors we live by*. Chicago, IL: University of Chicago Press.

Latta, M. M., & Kim, J. H. (2009). Narrative inquiry invites professional development: Educators claim the creative space of praxis. *Journal of Educational Research, 103*(2), 137–148.

Lindsay, G. M. (2006a). Experiencing nursing education research: Narrative inquiry and interpretive phenomenology. *Nurse Researcher, 13*(4), 30–38.

Lindsay, G. M. (2006b). Constructing a nursing identity: Reflecting on and reconstructing experience. *Reflective Practice, 7*(1), 59–72.

Miller, J. (1990). *Creating spaces and finding voices: Teachers collaborating for empowerment*. Albany, NY: State University of New York.

Murphy, M. S. (2011). Poetry from report cards: Children's understandings of themselves in relationship with their teachers. In C. Craig & L. Deretchin (Eds.), *Cultivating curious and creative minds: The role of teachers and teacher educators* (Vol. 2). Lanham, MD: Rowman & Littlefield.

Murray Orr, A. (2002). Book conversations as acts of caring: A teacher researcher's reflective engagement with Noddings' ethic of care. *Curriculum and Teaching Dialogue, 2*(1), 89–100.

Murray Orr, A., & Olson, M. (2007). Transforming narrative encounters. *Canadian Journal of Education, 30*(3), 819–838.

Olson, M. (1995). Conceptualizing narrative authority: Implications for teacher education. *Teaching and Teacher Education, 11*(2), 119–135.

Olson, M. (2000). Curriculum as a multistoried process. *Canadian Journal of Education, 25*(3), 169–187.

Olson, M. (2008). Valuing narrative authority, collaboration and diversity in revitalizing a teacher education program. In C. Craig & L. Deretchin (Eds.), *Imagining a renaissance in teacher education* (pp. 377–394). Lanham, MD: Rowman & Littlefield.

Olson, M., & Craig, C. (2001). Opportunities and challenges in the development of teachers' knowledge: The development of narrative authority through knowledge communities. *Teaching and Teacher Education, 17*(7), 667–684.

Olson, M., & Craig, C. (2005). Uncovering cover stories: Tensions and entailments in the development of teacher knowledge. *Curriculum Inquiry, 35*(2), 161–182.

Olson, M., & Craig, C. (2009a). Small stories and mega-stories: Accountability in balance. *Teachers College Record, 111*(2), 547–572.

Olson, M., & Craig, C. (2009b). Traveling stories: Converging milieus and educational conundrums. *Teaching and Teacher Education, 25*, 1077–1085.

Pedrana, A. (2009). Teachers of English language learners: Tracking personal practical knowledge, reflection, and narrative authority. *Curriculum and Teaching Dialogue, 11*(1/2), 175–191.

Phillion, J., & He, M. F. (2005). Narrative inquiry in English language training: Contributions and future directions. In J. Cummins & C. Davison (Eds.), *Handbook of English language teaching* (Vol. 2). The Netherlands: Kluwer Academic Publishing.

Phillion, J., He, M. F., & Connelly, F. M. (Eds.). (2005). *Narrative & experience in multicultural education*. Thousand Oaks, CA: Sage.

Pinnegar, S. (1995). (Re)experiencing beginning. *Teacher Education Quarterly, 22*(3), 65–84.

Pinnegar, S. (1996a). Sharing stories: A teacher educator accounting for narrative in her teaching. *Action in Teacher Education, 18*(3), 13–22.

Pinnegar, S. (1996b). Depending on experience. *Educational Research Quarterly, 21*(2), 43–59.

Pinnegar, S., & Daynes, J. G. (2006). Locating narrative inquiry historically: Thematics in the turn to narrative. In D. J. Clandinin (Ed.), *Handbook of narrative inquiry: Mapping a methodology* (pp. 3–34). Thousand Oaks, CA: Sage.

Polkinghorne, D. E. (1988). *Narrative knowing and the human sciences*. Albany, NY: State University of New York Press.

Pushor, D. (2011). Attending to milieu: Living a *Curriculum of Parents* alongside teacher candidates. In J. Kitchen, D. Parker & D. Pushor (Eds.), *Narrative inquiries into curriculum making in teacher education* (pp. 217–237). Bingley, UK: Emerald Group.

Rice, M. (2011). *Adolescent boys' literate identity*. Bingley, UK: Emerald Group.

Ross, V. (2003). Walking around the curriculum tree: An analysis of a third/fourth grade mathematics lesson. *Journal of Curriculum Studies, 35*(5), 567–584.

Ross, V. (2004). A story of reform: Math, science, technology investigation (MSI) in room 34 at Bay Street Community School. *The Journal of Curriculum Studies, 36*(5), 587–594.

Ross, V., & Chan, E. (2008). Multicultural education: Raj's story as a curricular conceptual lens of the particular. *Teaching and Teacher Education, 24*(7), 1705–1716.

Sack, J. (2008). Commonplace intersections within a high school mathematics leadership institute. *Journal of Teacher Education, 59*(2), 189–199.

Schlein, C. (2007). The temporal experience of curriculum. *Curriculum and Teaching Dialogue, 9*(1/2), 35–45.

Schlein, C. (2009). Exploring novice teachers' experiences with intercultural curriculum. *Journal of Curriculum Theorizing, 25*(3), 22–33.

Schön, D. (1983). *The reflective practitioner: How professionals think in action*. London: Temple Smith.

Schön, D. (1987). *Educating the reflective practitioner: How professionals think in action*. San Francisco, CA: Jossey-Bass.

Schön, D. (1991). *The reflective turn: How professionals think in and on educational practice*. New York, NY: Teachers College Press.

Schwab, J. J. (1954/1978). Eros and education: A discussion of one aspect of discussion. In I. Westbury & N. Wilkof (Eds.), *Science, curriculum and liberal education: Selected essays*. Chicago, IL: University of Chicago Press.

Schwab, J. J. (1969). The practical: A language for curriculum. *School Review, 78*, 1–23.

Schwab, J. J. (1971). The practical: Arts of the eclectic. *School Review, 79*, 493–542.

Schwab, J. J. (1973). The practical 3: Translation into curriculum. *School Review, 81*, 501–522.

Schwab, J. J. (1983). The practical 4: Something for curriculum professors to do. *Curriculum Inquiry, 13*(3), 239–265.
Seaman, M. (2008a). Birds of a feather? Communities of practice and knowledge communities. *Curriculum and Teaching Dialogue, 10*(1/2), 269–279.
Seaman, M. (2008b). *First-time teacher, second time around: A narrative self-study of teaching in higher education.* The Netherlands: VDM Verlag.

AFTERWORD: REFLECTIONS ON NARRATIVE INQUIRIES INTO TEACHER EDUCATION IDENTITY MAKING

D. Jean Clandinin

> Arguments for the development and use of narrative inquiry come out of a view of human experience in which humans, individually and socially, lead storied lives. People shape their daily lives by stories of who they and others are and as they interpret their past in terms of these stories. Story, in the current idiom, is a portal through which a person enters the world and by which his or her experience of the world is interpreted and made personally meaningful. Viewed this way, narrative is the phenomena studied in inquiry. Narrative inquiry, the study of experience as story, then, is first and foremost a way of thinking about experience. Narrative inquiry as methodology entails a view of the phenomena. To use narrative inquiry methodology is to adopt a particular view of experience as phenomena under study. (Connelly & Clandinin, 2006, p. 377)

While Michael Connelly and I wrote this definition of narrative inquiry in the early 2000s, it was some years earlier when we first turned our attention to questions of identity (Connelly & Clandinin, 1999). In the 1980s and 1990s we attended to what we called teachers' personal practical knowledge (Clandinin, 1986; Connelly & Clandinin, 1988) as embodied, narrative, emotional, moral knowledge which was expressed and lived out on what we saw as storied professional knowledge landscapes (Clandinin & Connelly, 1995, 1996). The storied professional knowledge landscape shaped the stories that teachers, and others, lived out on school contexts, and shaped the knowledge that teachers held in their bodies and expressed in their practices. We also knew that as teachers, and others, lived in those landscapes, their living knowledge shaped the knowledge landscapes. However, it was not until the teachers with whom we worked directed our attention to their wonders about who they were, and were becoming, that we began to attend to identity. As we worked alongside teachers in their classrooms and schools,

> we noticed that teachers seemed to be trying to answer different questions. Their questions were ones of identity. They were questions of "Who am I in my story of

teaching?"; "Who am I in my place in the school?"; "Who am I in children's stories?"; "Who am I in parents' stories?" and so on. We began to listen more closely. What we heard intrigued us. ... teachers were more inclined to ask questions along the lines of "Who am I in this situation?" than "What do I know in this situation?". (Connelly & Clandinin, 1999, p. 3)

As we continued in this work, "we realized that the theoretical puzzle was to link knowledge, context, and identity" (Connelly & Clandinin, 1999, p. 3). The concept we eventually developed was stories to live by, a term that helps us understand these ideas as linked narratively. The term, stories to live by,

is given meaning by the narrative understandings of knowledge and context. Stories to live by are shaped by such matters as secret teacher stories, sacred stories of schooling, and teachers' cover stories. (Connelly & Clandinin, 1999, p. 4)

As we engaged in our studies alongside teachers and administrators in schools in the 1980s and 1990s, we saw our work as shifting the scholarly conversations in teacher education and curriculum studies in ways that allowed us to view teachers as people expressing their personal practical knowledge within knowledge landscapes. We saw this as a radical shift from the earlier views of teachers, which mostly constructed them as appliers of theoretical knowledge, and as the weak link in curriculum reform efforts (Clandinin & Connelly, 1998). As we began to focus on linking knowledge and context through a narrative concept of identity, the scholarly conversation was shifting again to include teachers' identity making as linked to the processes of curriculum making.

As I read the chapters in this book, I see these authors are also shifting the conversation in teacher education as Michael and I did around teachers so many years ago. They are attending to what teacher educators are asking. They are, in this book, asking questions, not about teacher educators' knowledge, not about teacher educators' contexts, but questions about who they are, and who they are becoming, as teacher educators. This is an important shift as so many scholarly conversations in teacher education today are shaped by questions around the knowledge of teacher educators, the contexts of teacher educators, about who should we name as teacher educators, and so on. The questions being asked in this book are different questions. They are questions about who each of the authors are as teacher educators, who they are becoming. And their questions are ones that speak to the narrative links between personal practical knowledge and professional knowledge landscapes, links made by the narrative concept of stories to live by.

Afterword

These questions of identity are ones that live deeply within me as I try to think about who I am, and who I am becoming. I am, and I realize that I have been for a while now, that is, since I left teaching in schools, in the midst of composing a further life as I draw forward the title of Mary Catherine Bateson's latest book (Bateson, 2011). When I left my work in schools when and where I could think of myself easily as a teacher, I came to the university and began to try to fit into the stories of teacher educators. It has been a difficult journey to figure out who I am becoming, who I am not yet, and all the ways in which who I am becoming shifts in place, time, and relationship. I am, as Maxine Greene (1995) reminds me, not yet.

Uncomfortably perched on multiple landscapes – school, home, university – I feel settled in none of them. The landscapes filled with stories that position me in multiple plotlines make me feel that no one skin fits comfortably. Place and time and relationship all shape these stories to live by that are embodied in me. These multiple places where I live, and these multiple stories that I live and tell, are always shifting. Often the shifts are subtle, happening almost without my being awake to them. And my wonders about identity, my stories to live by that are me in the making and in the midst, were ideas that came with me as I thought about the chapters in this book.

As I read the chapters, I remembered some of David Morris' words. Morris, drawing on Keith Basso, wrote

> One Apache male describes how such tales, when retold in the context of moral misconduct, have a way of almost literally getting under your skin: "That story is working on you now. You keep thinking about it. That story is changing you now, making you want to live right. That story is making you want to replace yourself." (Morris, 2002, p. 197)

Usually this quote from Basso helps me think about the relational ethics of engaging in narrative inquiry. However, in reading the chapters in this book, Basso's quotation resonates in different ways. I think of what is happening to me, and to the authors of these chapters, as teacher educators who are composing lives in multiple places within dominant narratives composed of teacher educators. The stories in these chapters are working on me now, making me want to re-place myself.

In reading Dixie Keyes and Cheryl Craig's chapter, I wondered about what sustains me, what sustains my stories to live by, what carries me from day to day. I also wondered about what interrupts my stories to live by? What can shift and change my stories to live by? Are they interrupted in one context, and does that interruption shift them in other contexts? As I am interrupted or sustained, what is happening to my stories to live by, to who I am becoming, to who I am not becoming? These questions linger with me as I sit here at my kitchen table writing these words.

I am also wondering about how my early landscapes, what I knew first, shape my stories to live by. M. Shaun Murphy, Vicki Ross, and Janice Huber's chapter called me to think about my early stories to live by and to wonder about how they are lived out now in such radically different contexts. As I read their stories, I wondered, have my stories to live by altered so much? Have I been transformed from one set of stories to live by to another? Do those early familial stories, lived out in certain times and places, still shape who I am and who I am becoming? As I write this afterword in the midst of spring coming to northern Alberta, I think I am not so different now as I yearn to leave my computer, put on my rubber boots, and find where the snow has melted into streams of running water. I know that as a child I would have finished whatever responsibilities I had and have fled the house. Now I tell myself to finish this response, there will be no time later. Perhaps my stories to live by have shifted dramatically.

In reading the chapter by Stefinee Pinnegar and Mary Lynn Hamilton, my attention was drawn to how coming alongside students and colleagues in these shifting landscapes might interrupt, but also sustain, my stories to live by. As I read Stefinee's story of the young student who wondered if she "could talk about how I feel about it" and Mary Lynn's story of shutting the door to profess revolution, I thought about who I was, am, am becoming, as a teacher educator. I do not want to forget. I want to remember that I too was once that young teacher who wondered if I could talk about how I felt, and I was also that young teacher who shut the door to practice what Maxine Greene (1995) calls "otherwise" in her classroom. I want to be sustained, but I also want to be interrupted and reminded not to fall into complacency, to remember that beginning teachers are, like I was so long ago, trying to make educative spaces for children in schools. Are their landscapes so constrained, so filled with dominant narratives, that this is no longer possible? I watch so many of them leave teaching. I wonder, were their stories to live by interrupted so sharply that they became stories to leave by (Clandinin, Downey, & Huber, 2009) too soon.

Candice Schlein and Elaine Chan's chapter called me to attend to the familial and cultural narratives in which all of our stories are embedded, and which shaped our living and becoming. I know that my stories to live by are being shaped in so many ways, ways that no matter how hard I try, I am not awake to. I wake up slowly, over time, over place, over relationships.

Afterword

Working alongside students whose lives are nested in different, and differing, cultural narratives, becoming a grandmother to a beautiful little boy and wondering if he will be labeled "mixed race" by those who work in schools and how that will influence the stories he lives by, and working in an afterschool arts program with youth labeled "Aboriginal" awakens me again to how much has changed in who I am, and am becoming. I could not, as a young student teacher, or even as a young teacher, have imagined becoming a teacher educator whose stories to live by have been so shifted. And yet, how do those shifts, those interruptions, those sustaining moments, happen? How can I give an account of them, so subtle they seem?

Mary Rice and Cathy Coulter's chapter reminded me that embodied knowing, what the body remembers, is intimately linked to storied contexts, and to our stories to live by. As Mary tells of multiple pathways and Cathy tells of being stopped in her busy tracks by the officer for speeding, I am reminded that these are our bodies, bodies that remember and know other times and places if we can slow down to listen to them. And again I look out the window on our farm and remember another long ago farm where Sunday was a time to go and play in the melting spring snow, to wade in the creeks that emerged in the warm sun from seemingly nowhere.

Reading this book reminds me of the complexity of what we are doing as narrative inquirers when we begin to inquire into who we are, and are becoming, as teacher educators. I end this foreword with a quotation from Ben Okri, quoted in Thomas King's book *The Truth about Stories*.

> In a fractured age,
> when cynicism is god,
> here it is a possibly heresy:
> we live by stories,
> we also live in them.
> One way or another we are living the stories
> planted in us early or along the way,
> or we are also living the stories we planted –
> knowingly or unknowingly – in ourselves
> We live stories that either give our lives meaning
> or negate it with meaninglessness.
> If we change the stories we live by,
> Quite possibly we change our lives.
> (Okri, as cited in King, 2003, p. 153)

"We live by stories" (Okri, as cited in King, 2003, p. 153) as teacher educators. We can know our lives, our practices, who we are, and are becoming, by attending to these stories. And it is through engaging in narrative inquiry with attention to working within the three-dimensional narrative inquiry space that we can come to understand who we are, and who we are becoming, as teacher educators.

As debates swirl around the globe about teacher education, it is important that we continue to inquire deeply and narratively into who we are, and are becoming. It is in this way that we can more fully, and more thoughtfully, engage with the preservice teachers who come to learn with us about who they are, and are becoming, as teachers. It is in this way that we can more fully, and more thoughtfully, engage in the policy discussions about teacher education.

REFERENCES

Bateson, M. C. (2011). *Composing a further life: The age of active wisdom*. New York, NY: Vintage Books.
Clandinin, D. J. (1986). *Teacher images: Teacher knowledge in action*. London: Falmer Press.
Clandinin, D. J., & Connelly, F. M. (1995). *Teachers professional knowledge landscapes*. New York, NY: Teachers College Press.
Clandinin, D. J., & Connelly, F. M. (1996). Teachers' professional knowledge landscapes: Teacher stories–stories of teachers–school stories–stories of school. *Educational Researcher, 25*(3), 24–30.
Clandinin, D. J., & Connelly, F. M. (1998). Stories to live by: Narrative understandings of school reform. *Curriculum Inquiry, 28*(2), 149–164.
Clandinin, D. J., Downey, C. A., & Huber, J. (2009). Attending to changing landscapes: Shaping the interwoven identities of teachers and teacher educators. *Asia-Pacific Journal of Teacher Education, 37*(2), 141–154.
Connelly, F. M., & Clandinin, D. J. (1988). *Teachers as curriculum planners: Narratives of experience*. New York, NY: Teachers College Press.
Connelly, F. M., & Clandinin, D. J. (1999). *Shaping a professional identity: Stories of educational practice*. New York, NY: Teachers College Press.
Connelly, F. M., & Clandinin, D. J. (2006). Narrative inquiry. In J. Green, G. Camili & P. Elmore (Eds.), *Handbook of complementary methods in education research* (pp. 375–385). Mahwah, NJ: Lawrence Erlbaum.
Greene, M. (1995). *Releasing the imagination: Essays on education, the arts, and social change*. San Francisco, CA: Jossey-Bass Inc.
King, T. (2003). *The truth about stories: A Native narrative*. Toronto, ON: House of Anansi Press Inc.
Morris, D. B. (2002). Narrative, ethics, and pain: Thinking with stories. In R. Charon & M. Montello (Eds.), *Stories matter: The role of narrative in medical ethics* (pp. 196–218). New York, NY: Routledge.

ABOUT THE CONTRIBUTORS

Elaine Chan is a teacher educator in the Department of Teaching, Learning, and Teacher Education, University of Nebraska-Lincoln, where she teaches undergraduate courses in Multicultural Education and graduate courses in diversity, Curriculum Studies, and research methodology. She was an elementary level teacher in Canada and in Japan, and has conducted research in Canadian, American, and Japanese schools. Her research focuses on ways children, teachers, and families experience school curriculum, and ways in which identity, culture, and curriculum intersect on school landscapes in transition. She is coauthor of the book, *Teaching the Arts to Engage English Language Learners* with Margaret Macintyre Latta.

D. Jean Clandinin is professor and director, Centre for Research for Teacher Education and Development, University of Alberta. A former teacher, counselor, and psychologist, she coauthored with F. Michael Connelly four books and many chapters and articles. Their most recent book is *Narrative Inquiry: Experience and Story in Qualitative Research*. Jean also co-authored a 2006 book entitled *Composing Diverse Identities*. Jean edited the *Handbook of Narrative Inquiry: Mapping a Methodology* (Sage, 2007).

Cathy Coulter is associate professor in the Department of Teaching and Learning at University of Alaska Anchorage. She is currently cochair of the Narrative Research SIG of the American Educational Research Association (AERA). Her research focuses on narrative research methodologies and the experiences of English learners, immigrant children, and indigenous children in public schools. Her articles are featured in journals such as *Educational Researcher*, *Curriculum Inquiry*, and *Bilingual Research Journal*.

Cheryl Craig is a professor in the College of Education at the University of Houston and coordinator of the teaching and teacher education program area. Her narrative inquiries have to do with how teachers' knowledge is shaped in context. She is executive editor of *Teachers and Teaching: Theory and Practice*, coeditor of the *American Teacher Educators' Yearbook*, and secretary of the International Association of Teachers and Teaching. In 2011, she was named an American Educational Research Association Fellow.

ABOUT THE CONTRIBUTORS

Mary Lynn Hamilton, professor in curriculum and teaching, University of Kansas, is a coeditor of *Teaching and Teacher Education*, an *International Journal of Research and Studies*. With Stefinee Pinnegar she has coauthored *Self-Study of Practice as a Genre of Qualitative Research: Theory, Methodology, and Practice*. Her research focuses on the development of teachers' professional knowledge and the research methodologies that make explicit the development of professional knowledge.

Janice Huber is associate professor in preservice and graduate teacher education at the University of Regina. She is a former elementary teacher and teacher researcher who, with Karen Keats Whelan, coauthored a relational, paper-formatted doctoral dissertation. Growing from doctoral and post doctoral study, Janice's collaborative narrative inquiries and publications, including the award winning book, *Composing Diverse Identities: Narrative Inquiries into the Interwoven Lives of Children and Teachers*, continue to explore narrative understandings of identity in relation with Aboriginal teachers and Elders in Canada and in relation with the curriculum-, identity-, and assessment-making experiences of children, families, and teachers. She is the 2006 recipient of the Narrative Research SIG (AERA) Early Career Award.

Dixie Keyes is an associate professor in the Department of Teacher Education at Arkansas State University in Jonesboro, Arkansas. Dixie is a teacher educator who lives alongside preservice teachers, inservice teachers, and graduate students with particular narrative inquiry research interests in teacher knowledge, teacher curriculum-making, issues of critical literacy, and adolescent literacy. She taught middle and high school English language arts for 15 years in Deep South Texas before beginning a career in higher education. She is active in state organizations and curriculum policy, and she directs the Arkansas Delta Writing Project, a National Writing Project site.

M. Shaun Murphy is associate professor at the University of Saskatchewan. He is a member of the Department of Curriculum Studies where he teaches mathematics methods in the undergraduate program and curriculum and methodology courses in the graduate program. He was a primary school teacher for twenty years in urban and rural settings. His research focuses on the ways children, teachers, and families cocompose curriculum and the ways this cocomposition is tied to identity making and assessment making. He also does research alongside beginning teachers. He was a coauthor on, *Composing Diverse Identities: Narrative Inquiries into the Interwoven Lives of Children and Teachers*, which received awards for its work on curriculum and narrative methodology. He has received teaching awards and is recognized for his work alongside student teachers.

About the Contributors

Stefinee Pinnegar, teacher educator in the McKay School of Education at Brigham Young University, began her teaching career working on the Navajo Reservation in Arizona. She received her Ph.D. from the University of Arizona. She and a group of her fellow graduate students (the Arizona Group) were founders of the Self-Study in Teacher Education Practices research movement. As acting dean of the Invisible College for Research on Teaching, she is concerned with developing conversations about research on teaching and teacher education. She is most interested in what and how teachers know as teachers and the research methodologies, such as self-study and narrative, that allow investigation in tacit memory and practical knowledge. She has published in the areas of teacher education, narrative, and self-study research and research methodology.

Mary Rice has published and presented nationally and internationally across a wide range of disciplines utilizing the methodology of narrative. These disciplines include folklore, geography, women's studies, literacy, linguistics, and teacher education. She has written chapters in books such as *A Geographical History of United States City-Systems: From the Frontier to Urban Transformation* (Edwin Mellen, 2004) and *Women Writing on Family: Tips on Writing, Teaching and Publishing* (Key, 2012). Her single-author book *Adolescent Boys' Literate Identity* (Emerald, 2011) is volume 15 in the *Advances in Research on Teaching* series. Her research interests include teacher thinking about literacy, advocacy for English learners in American schools, narrative and arts-based approaches to research, and self-study of teacher education practices.

Vicki Ross is associate professor at Northern Arizona University. She is a former elementary school teacher and is currently a member of the Department of Teaching and Learning where she primarily teaches mathematics methods in the undergraduate program and curriculum courses in the graduate program. She is recognized for outstanding teaching. Her research interests are in the area of mathematics education, teacher development, narrative inquiry, and curriculum.

Candace Schlein is assistant professor of curriculum studies, director of the master of arts in curriculum and instruction – general degree program, and director of the educational specialist in curriculum and instruction degree program at the School of Education of the University of Missouri–Kansas City. Her research interests include cross-cultural teaching and learning, diversity and social justice in education, curriculum, and narrative inquiry.